Sigils and Talismans of The Gallery of Magick

Printed Sigils and Talismans for Magickal Workers

Damon Brand

Disclaimer: Consider all information in this book to be speculation and not professional advice, to be used at your own risk. Damon Brand and The Gallery of Magick are not responsible for the consequences of your actions. The information is never intended to replace or substitute for medical advice from a professional practitioner, and when it comes to issues of physical health, mental health or emotional conditions, no advice is given or implied, and you should always seek conventional, professional advice. The information is provided on the understanding that you will use it in accordance with the laws of your country.

CONTENTS

Introduction: Cut Up the Book

This book contains sigils, seals and talismans from four Damon Brand books. It is only of use to you if you are familiar with these works, and if you want physical copies of these sigils. There are sigils from *The 72 Angels of Magick, Magickal Riches, Magickal Protection* and *Magickal Cashbook.* There are some practical benefits to be obtained by owning physical copies of these sigils, with some appearing in color, for example.

This book is not essential for all magickal workers. Some of the images can be download from the website, or people are happy to use the sigils on an iPad, computer screen or other color device, or to simply use the printed books. That suits them perfectly.

This book is designed for people who *want* access to the physical sigils. I produced this book because many people asked me to do so, and because this is the only way to get color versions of the physical sigils.

In an earlier version of this book, I also provided sigils from *The Magickal Job Seeker* and *Words of Power.* This book is printed in color, and the cost of color printing is extremely high, meaning the original version was not very cost-effective for the reader (costing almost US$60), even though there were many non-color sigils. The logical solution was to remove everything non-essential, to keep the cost down for you.

If you want physical copies of the sigils from *Words of Power* and *The Magickal Job Seeker*, or any of our other books, it is more efficient for you to purchase those books separately and photocopy (or photograph and print) the pages you require.

It is true that the sigils from *Magickal Protection* and several from *Magickal Riches* are not color, but I know that people often like to have physical copies with them, so they have been retained in this version of the book.

The main reason people buy this book is to obtain physical copies of the angelic sigils, complete with the red angelic seal at the center of the image. All seventy-two sigils from *The 72 Angels of Magick* are included, along with the shem talisman; that makes the work much easier to perform. (If you purchased *Magickal Angels* or *The Greater Magickal Angels* some years ago, those books have now been combined and up-dated into a single volume called *The 72 Angels of Magick.)*

There are three ways to use this book.

1. Use the images in the book by turning to the page, performing the ritual as described in the original text and then leaving the image in place by closing the book.

2. Photocopy the required images and use them in rituals. Even if you are using the first method, you may need to make some photocopies, as some rituals require two or more sigils and talismans to be used at once.

3. Cut up the book. This is why we designed the book with blank pages behind each image. You can cut out each page and use it as a sigil, seal or talisman. This book is not a holy relic, so there's no harm in breaking the spine and pulling out all the pages you want. Just be careful not to tear them as you pull the book apart. To be on the safe side, you may want to photocopy them first, so you have copies ready, just in case.

Once you've cut or torn out a page you can use the images in whatever way you want. You can cut out the shapes exactly, or cut out a rough shape around the main image, or use the whole page. It's entirely up to you and the way of working that you enjoy.

Damon Brand

www.galleryofmagick.com

Images from *The 72 Angels of Magick*

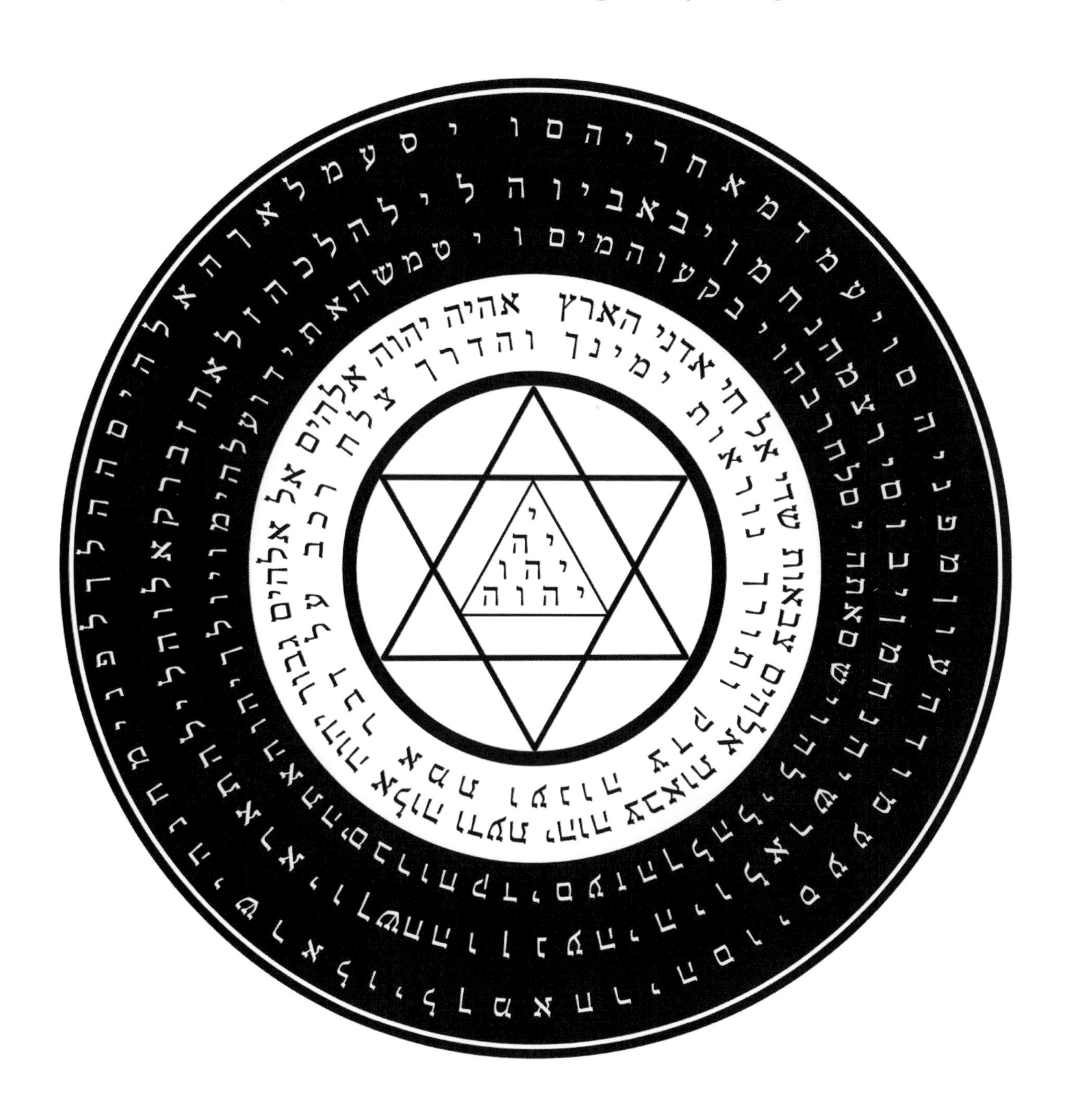

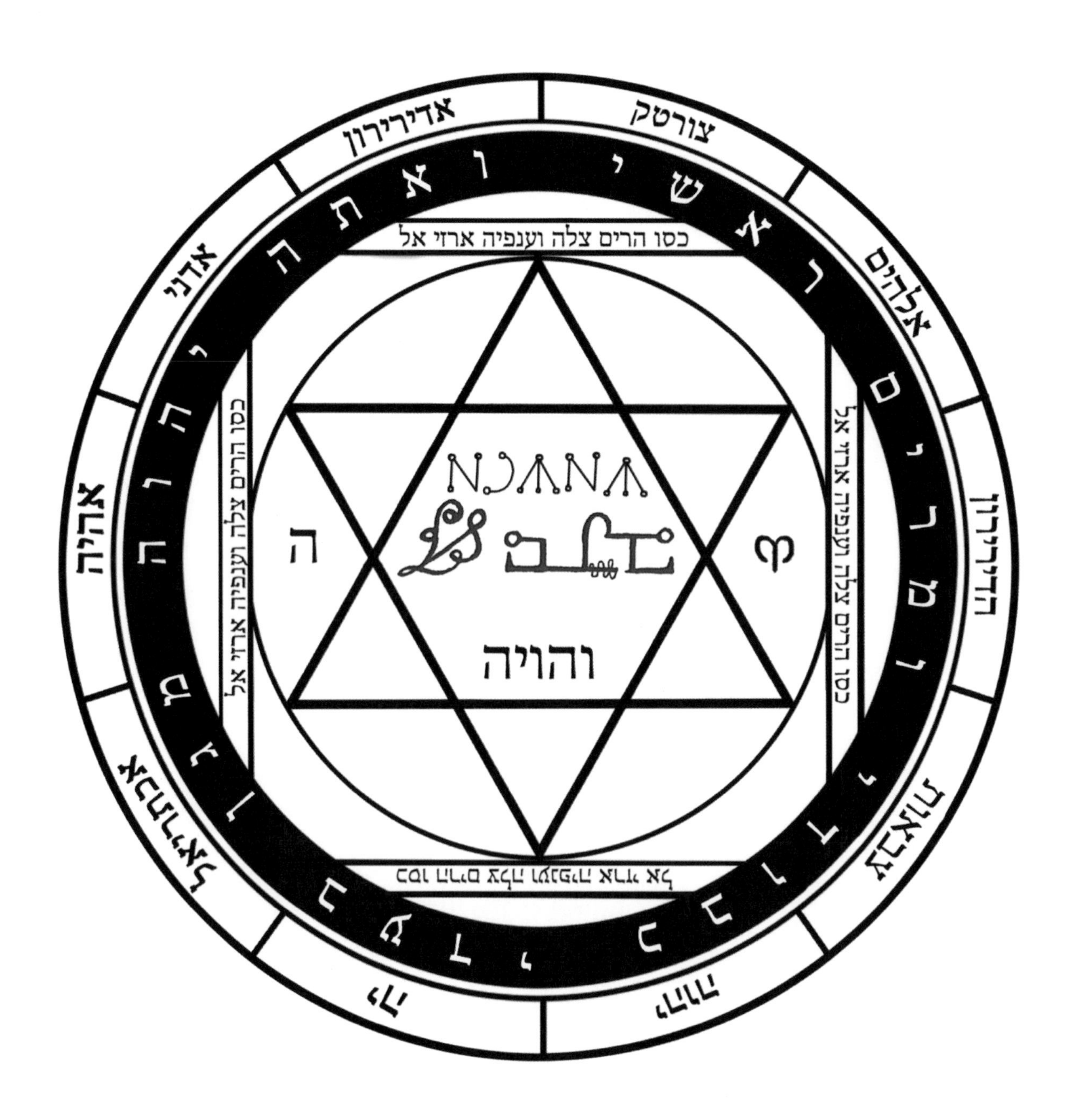

Vehuiah

VEH-WHO-EE-AH

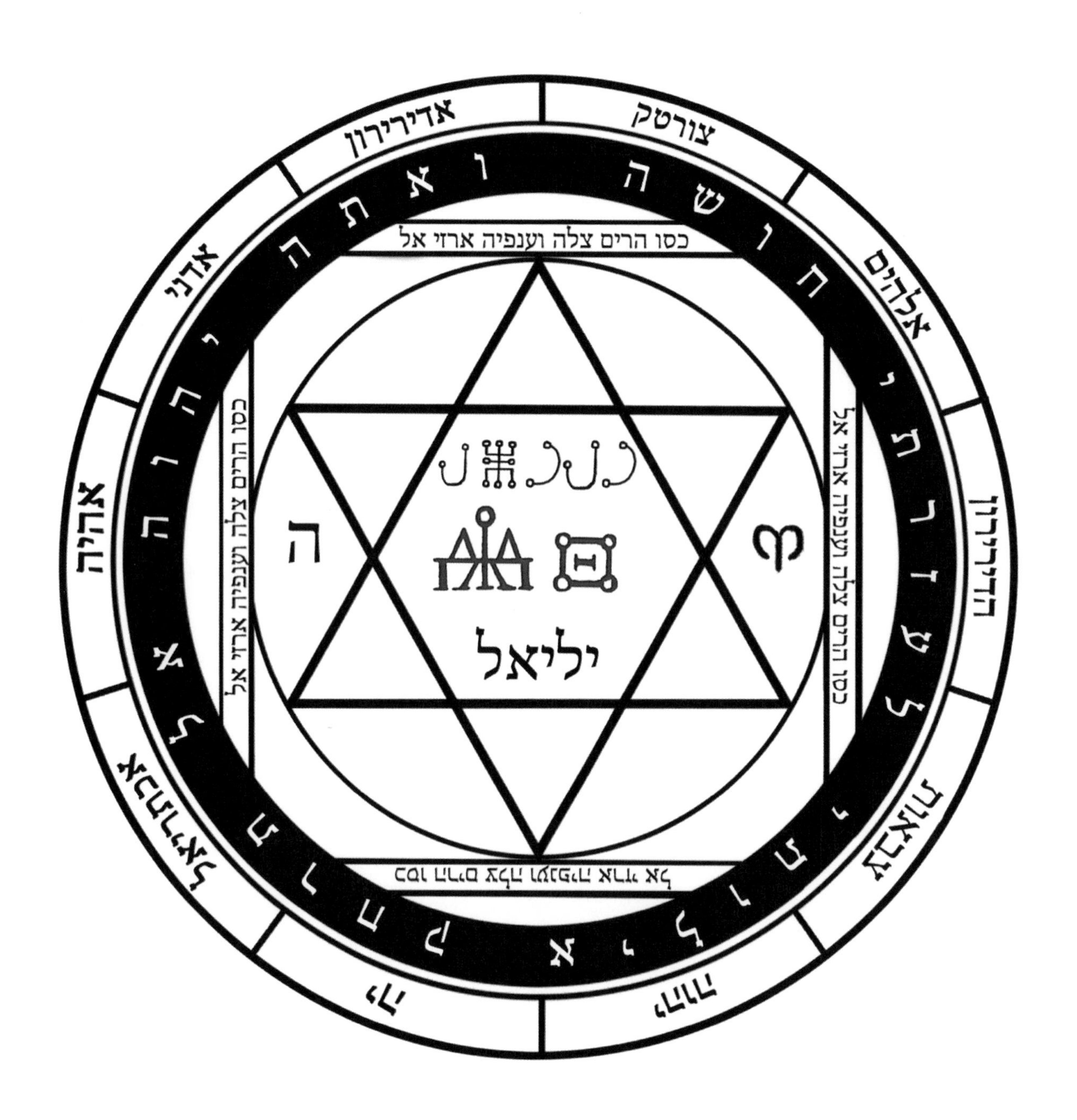

Yeliel

YEH-LEE-ELL

Sitael

SIT-AH-ELL

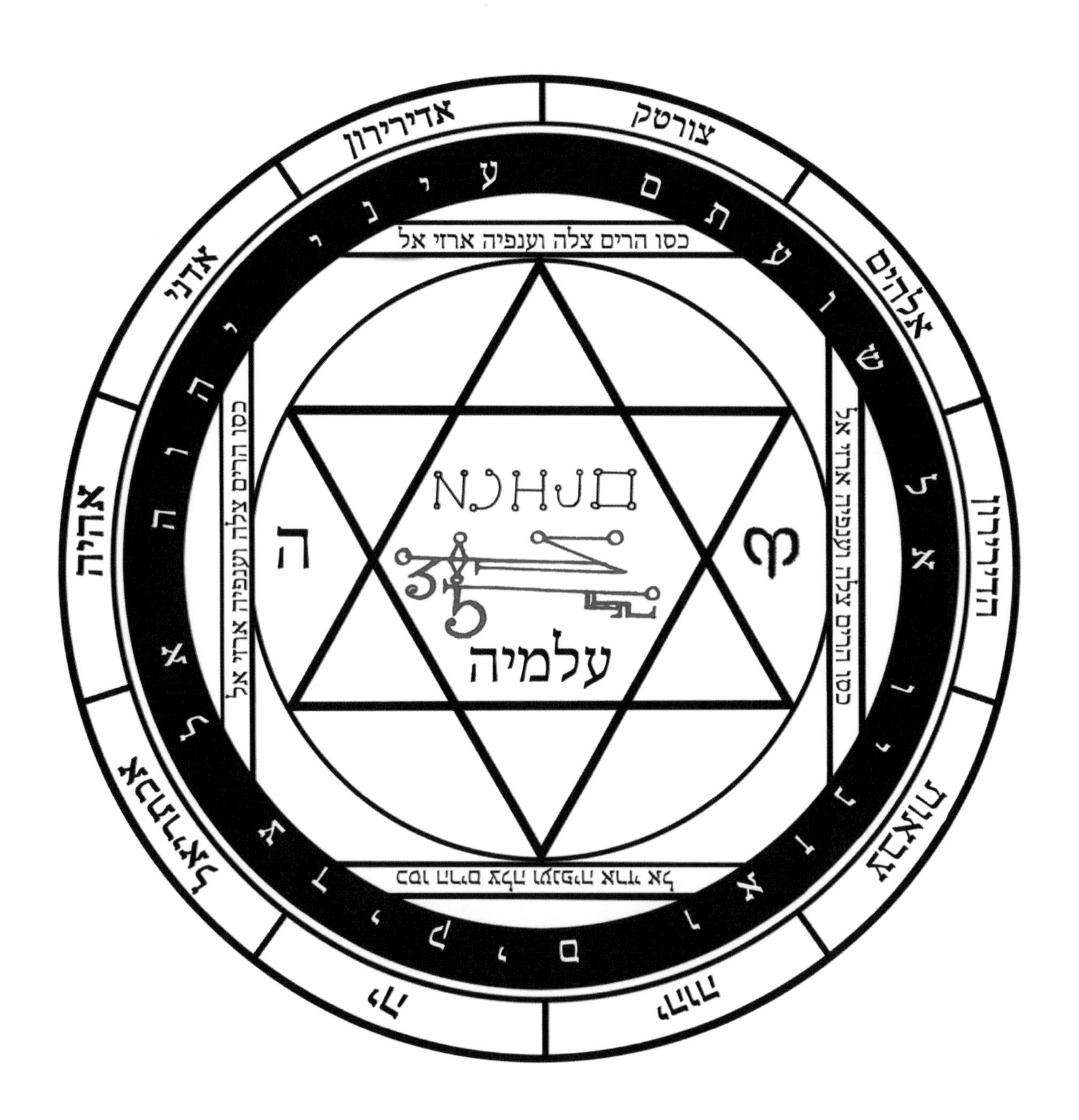

Elemiah

ELL-EM-EE-AH

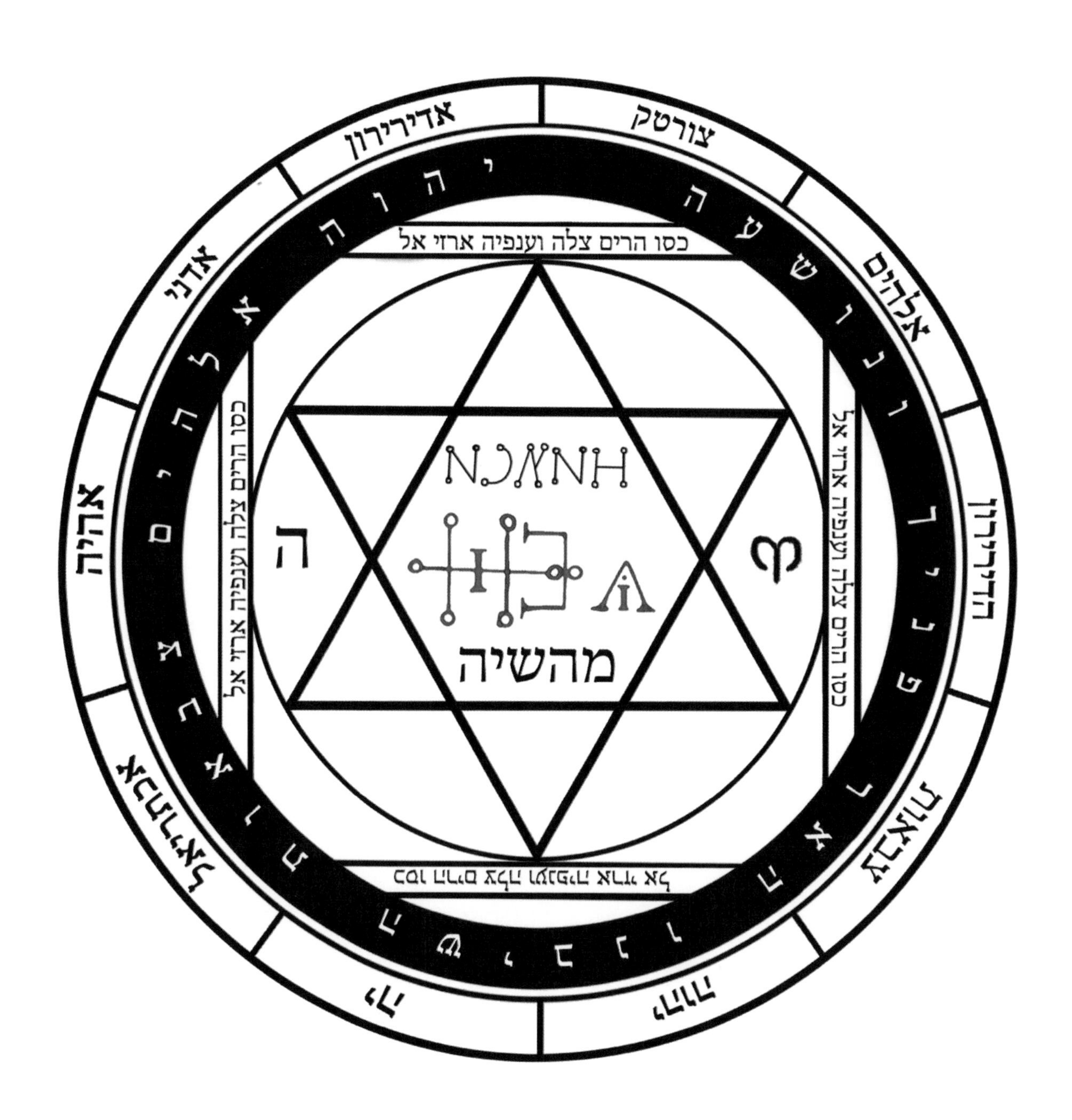

Mahasiah

MAH-HA-SHE-AH

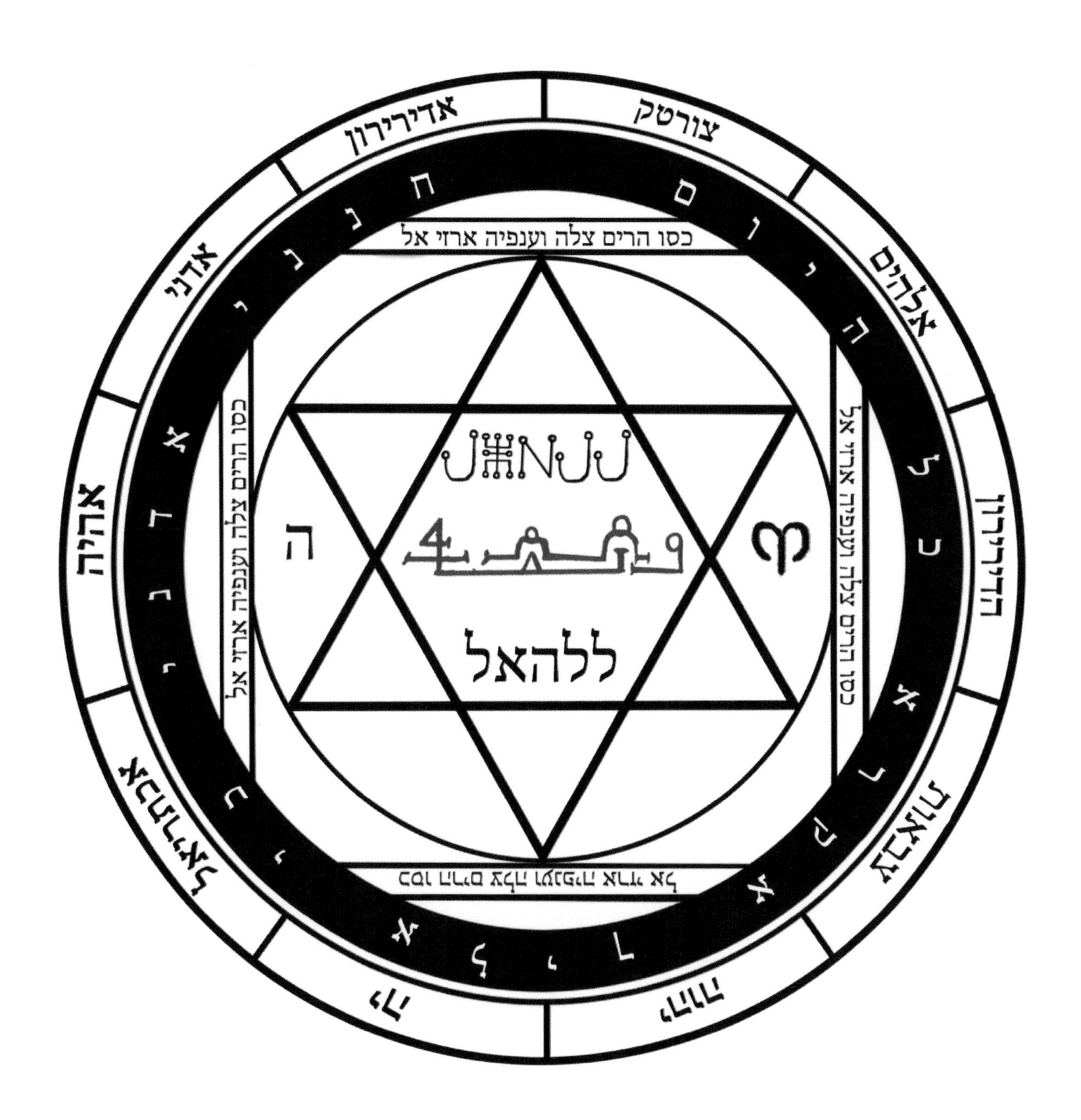

Lelahel

LEH-LAH-ELL

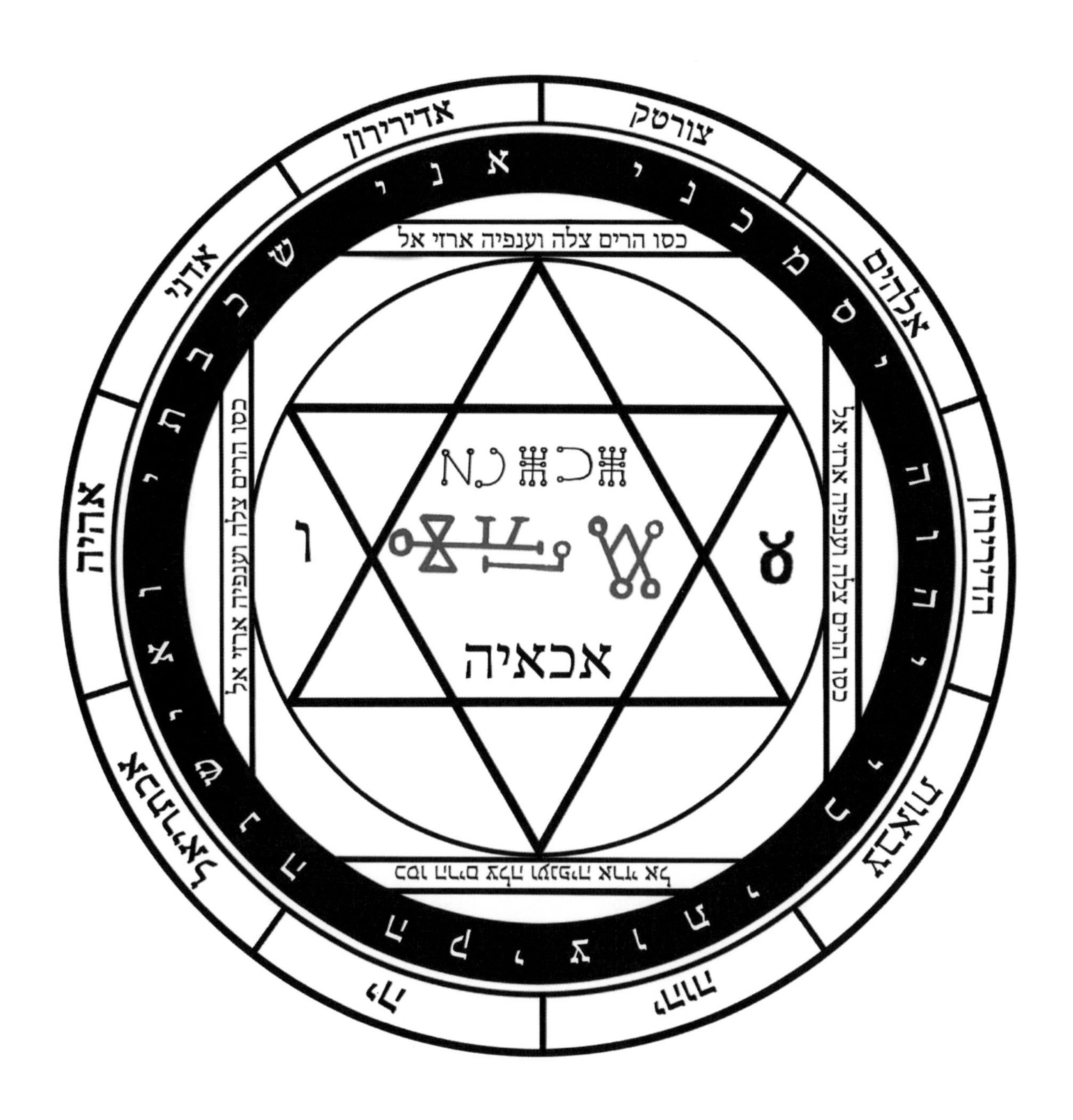

Achaiah

AH-CHAH-EE-YAH

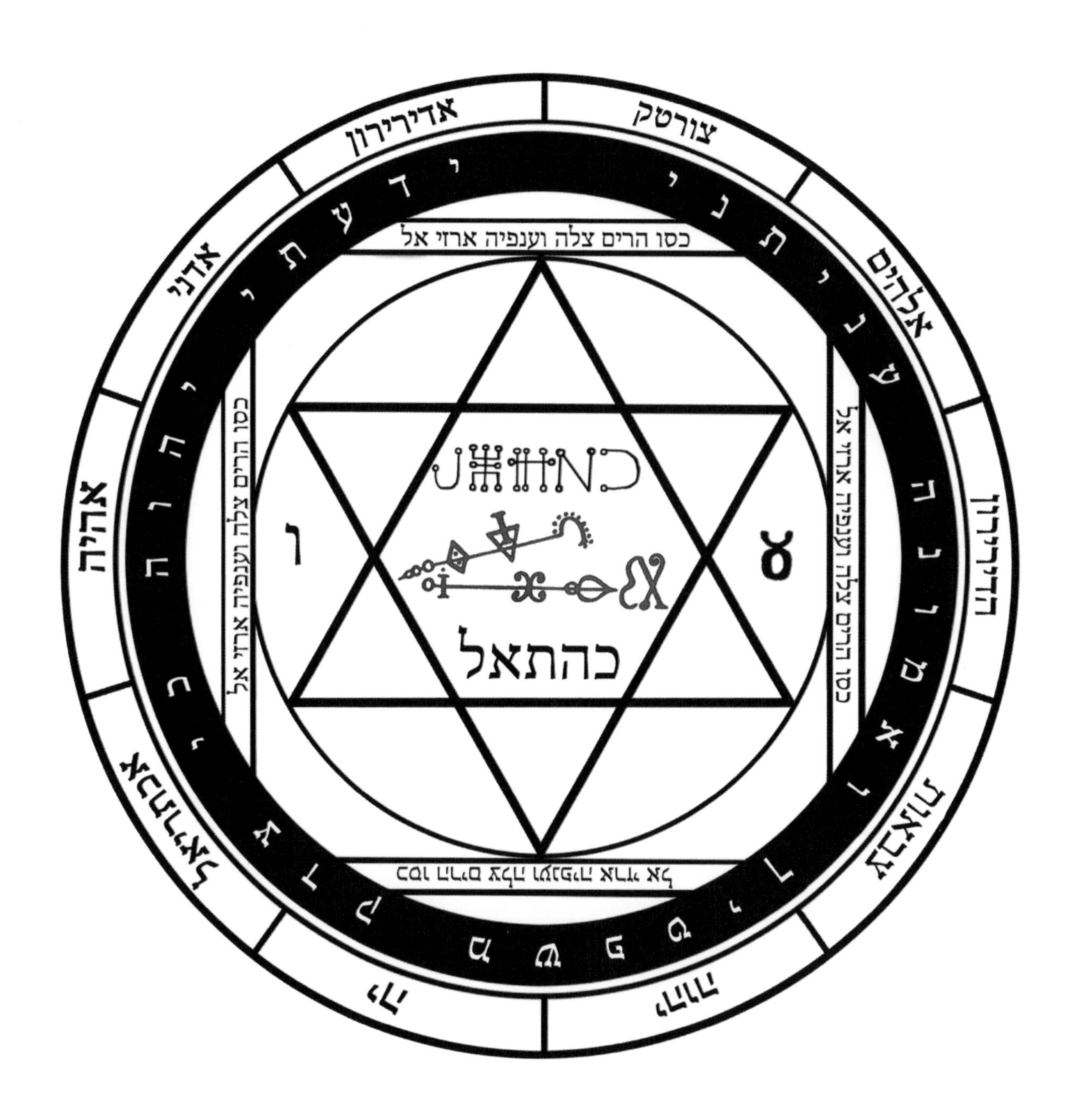

Cahetel

CAH-HET-ELL

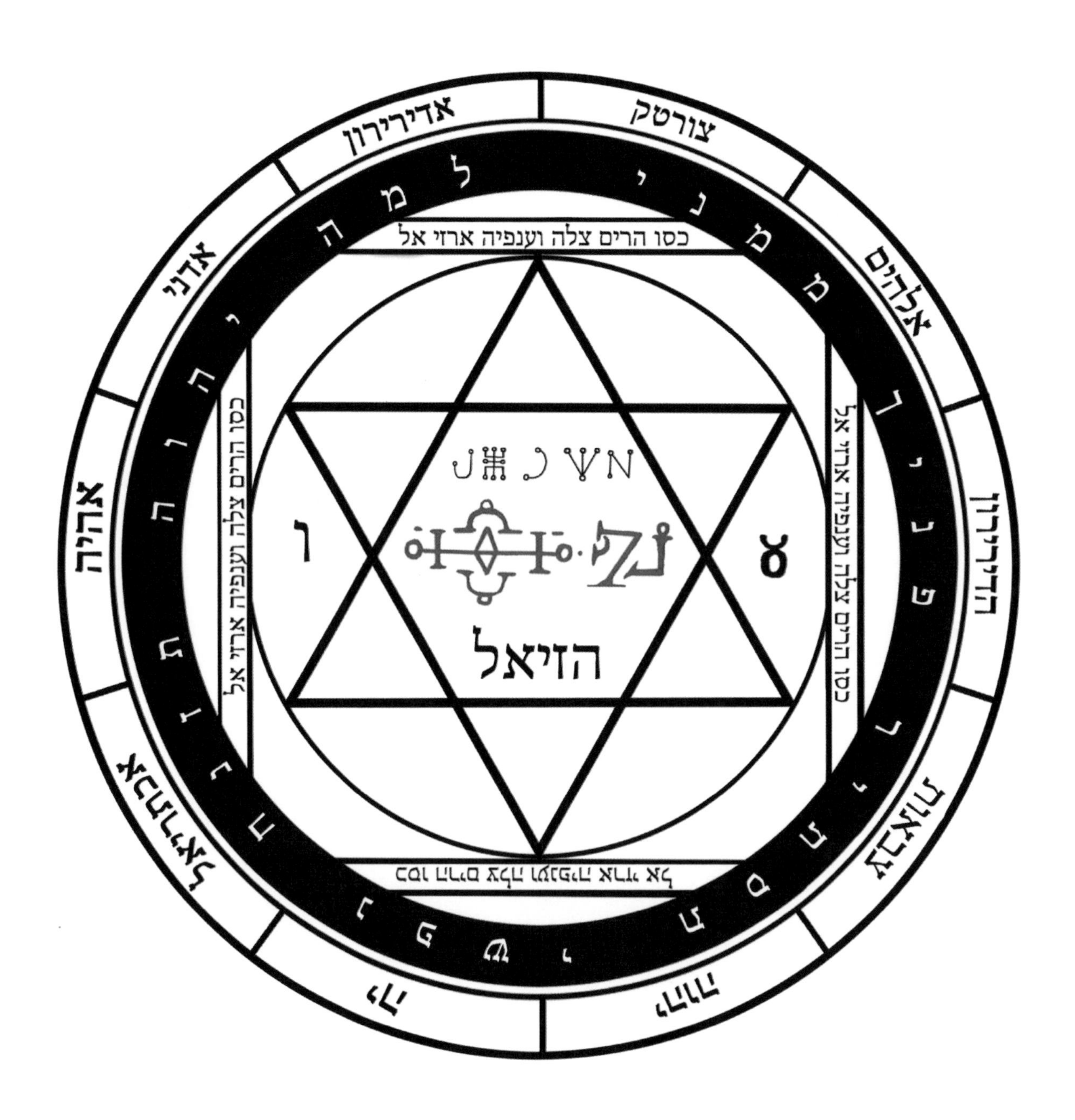

Heziel

HEZ-EE-ELL

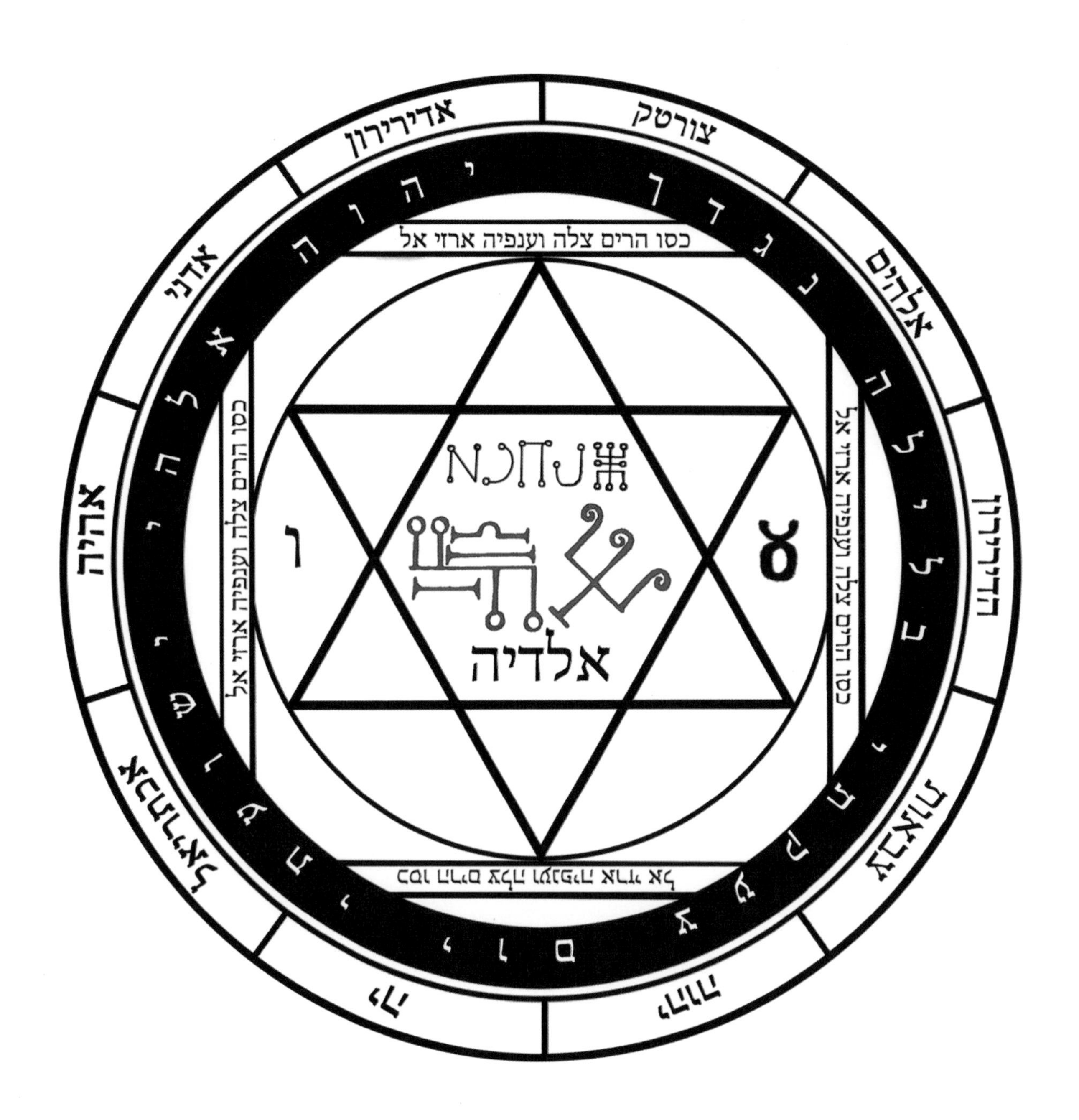

Eladiah

EH-LAH-DEE-YAH

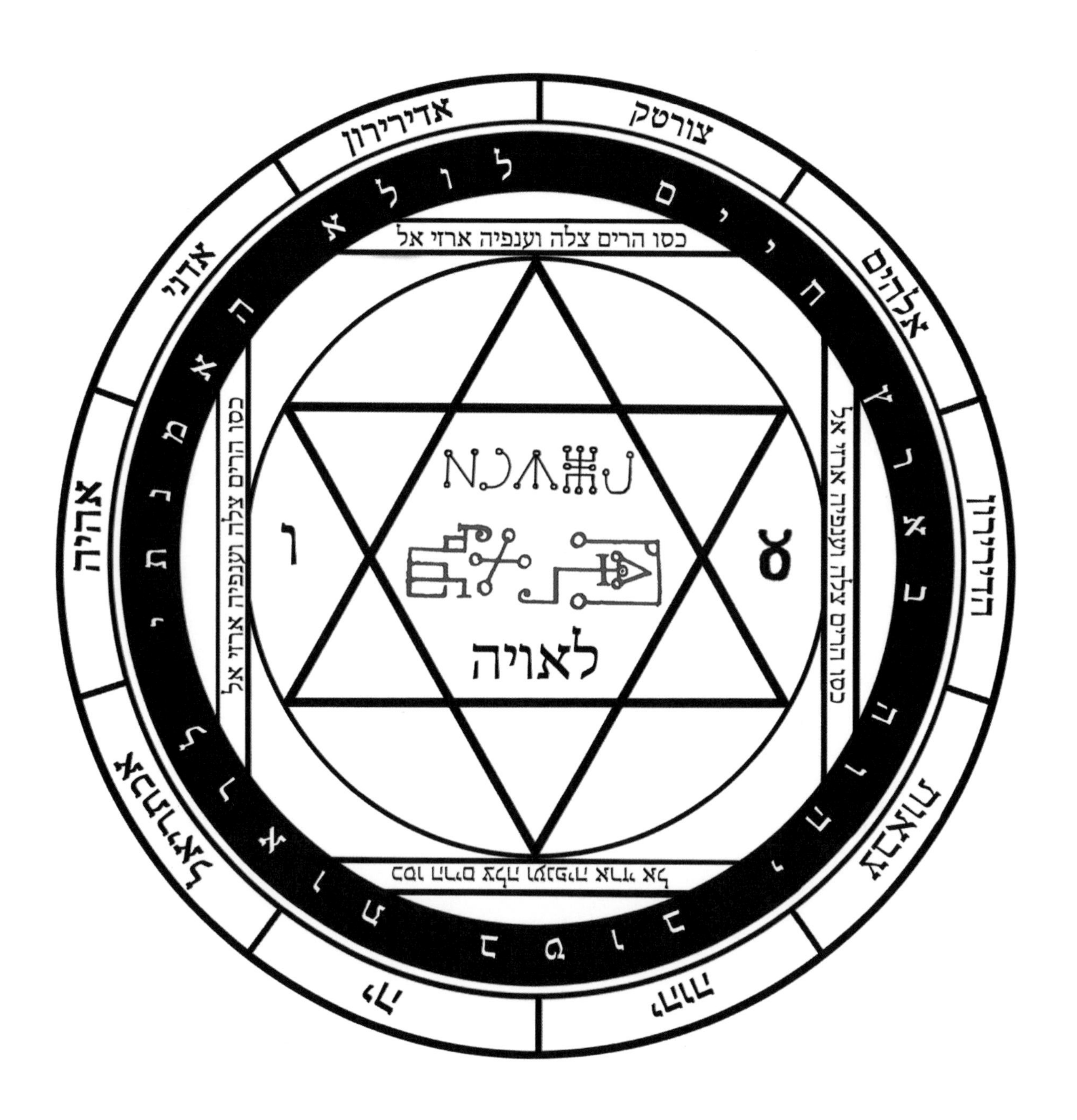

Laviah

LAH-VEE-AH

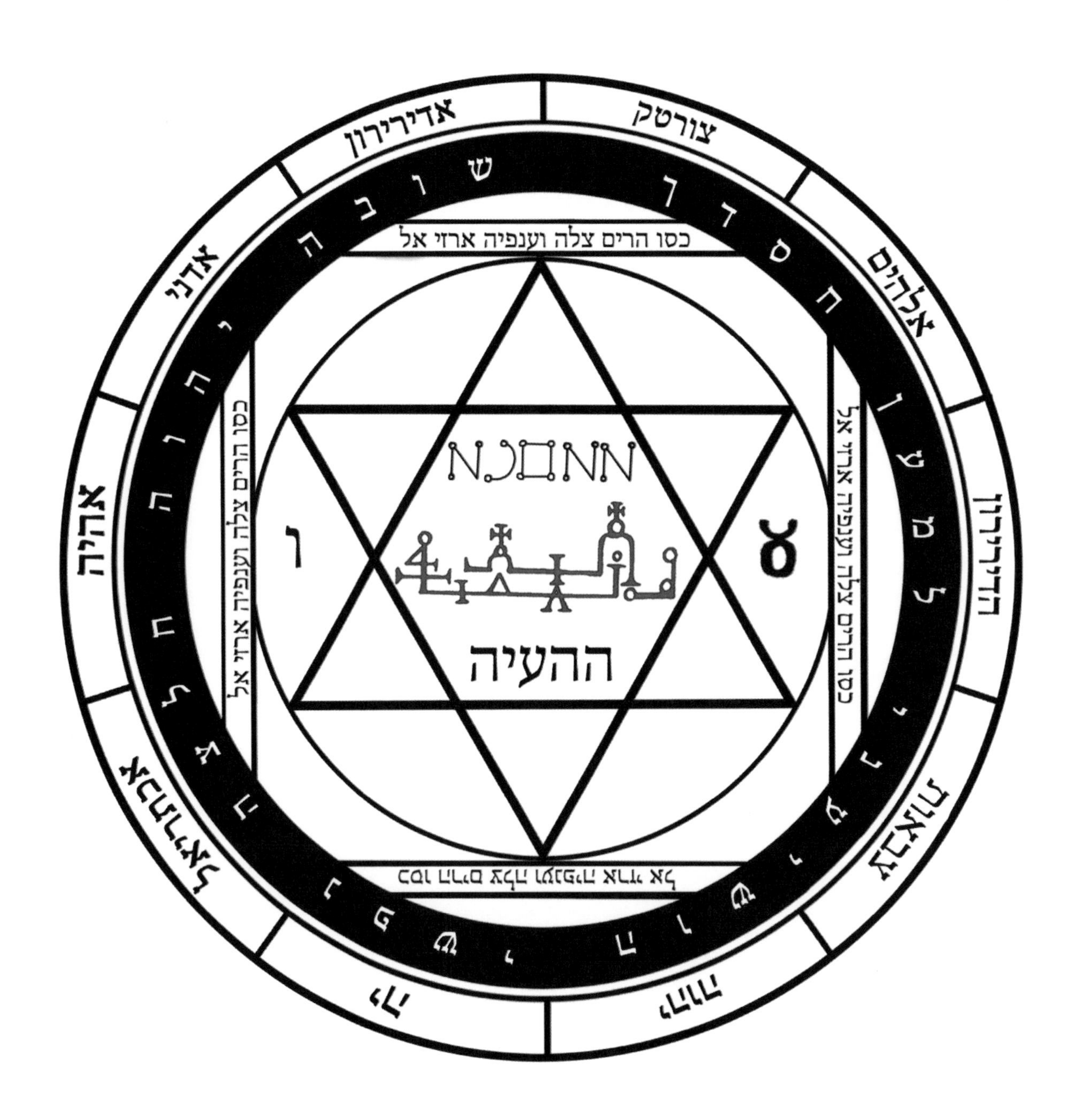

Hahaiah

HAH-HAH-EE-AH

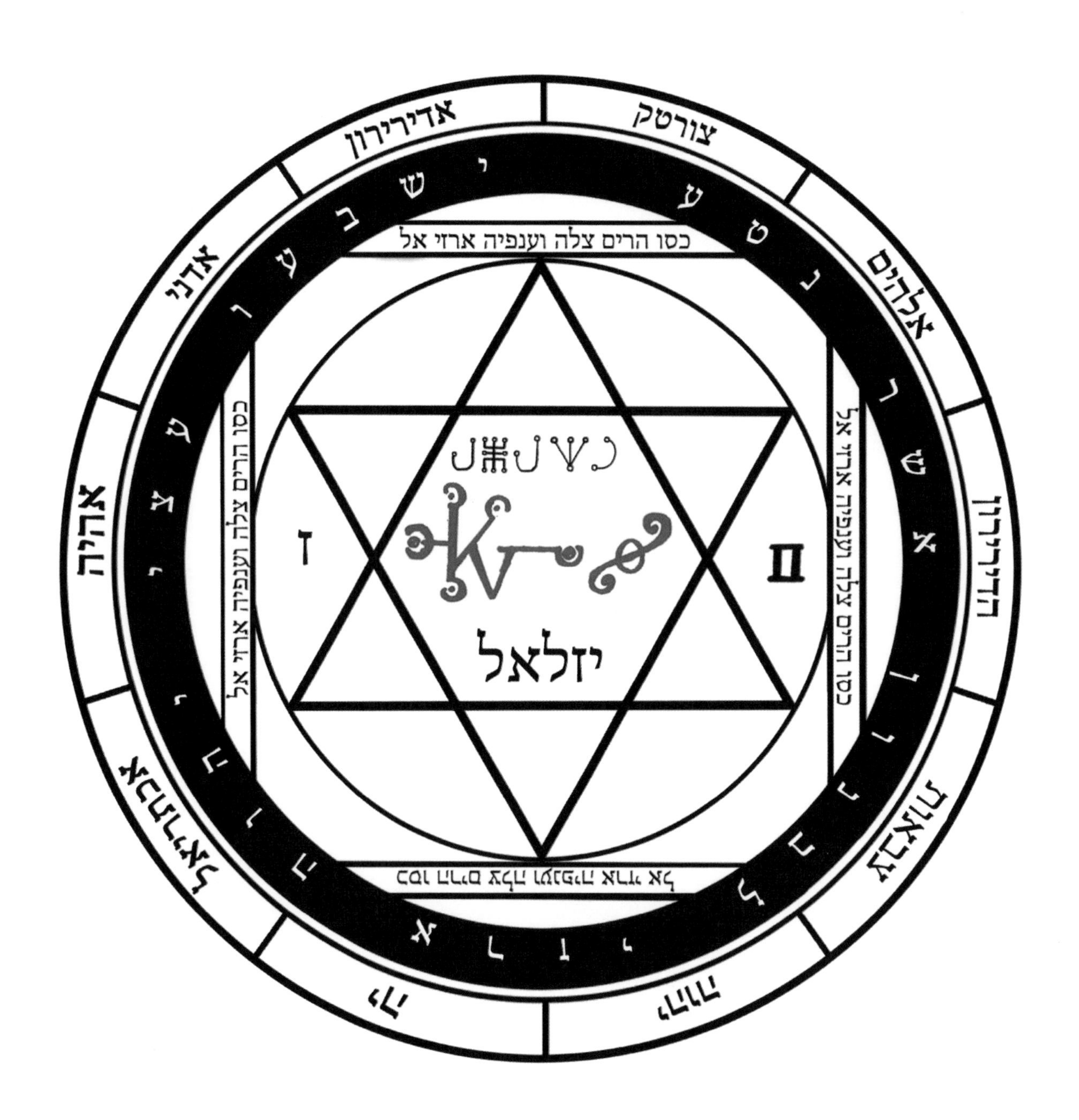

Yezelel

YEH-ZELL-ELL

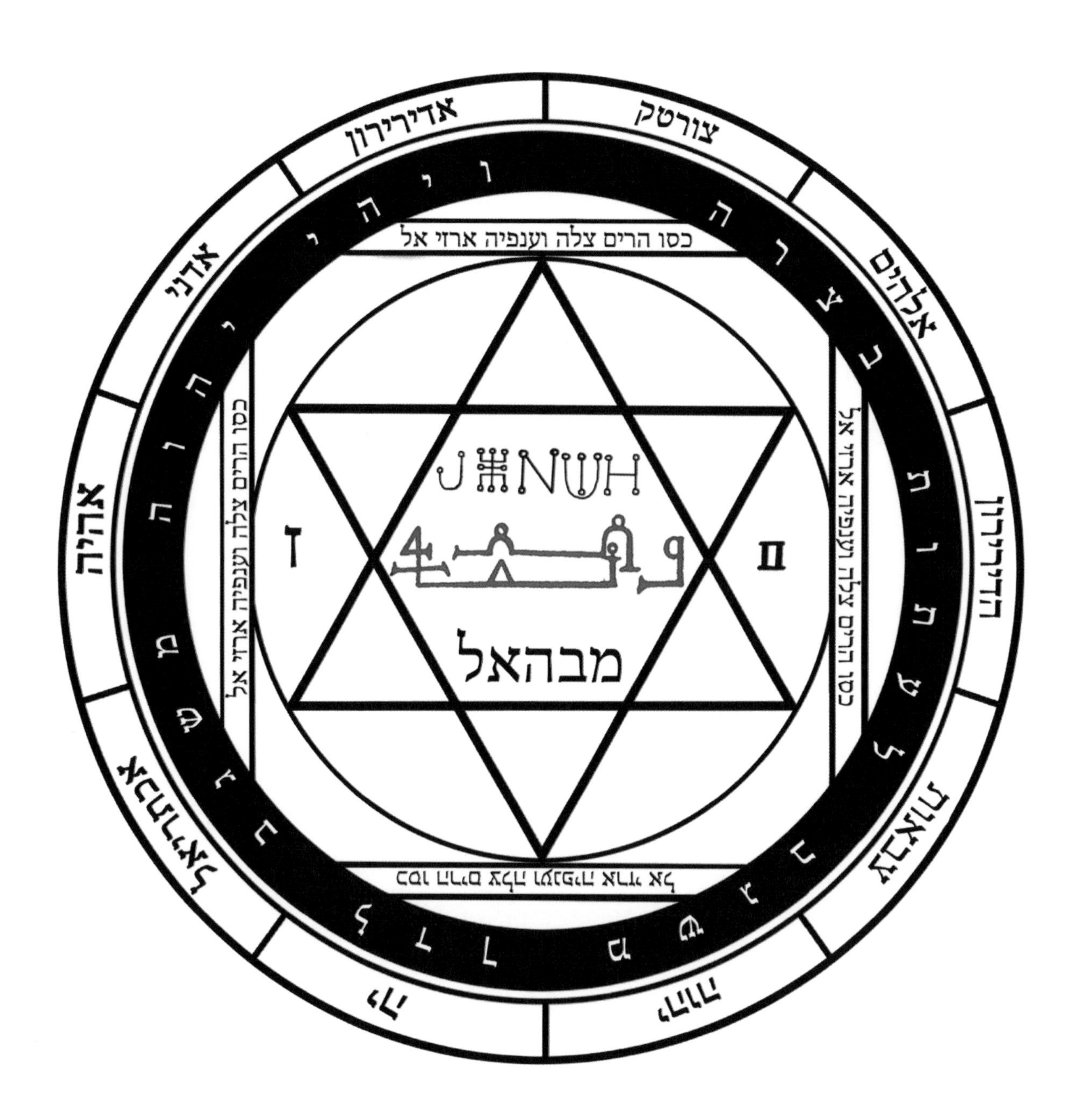

Mebahel

MEB-AH-ELL

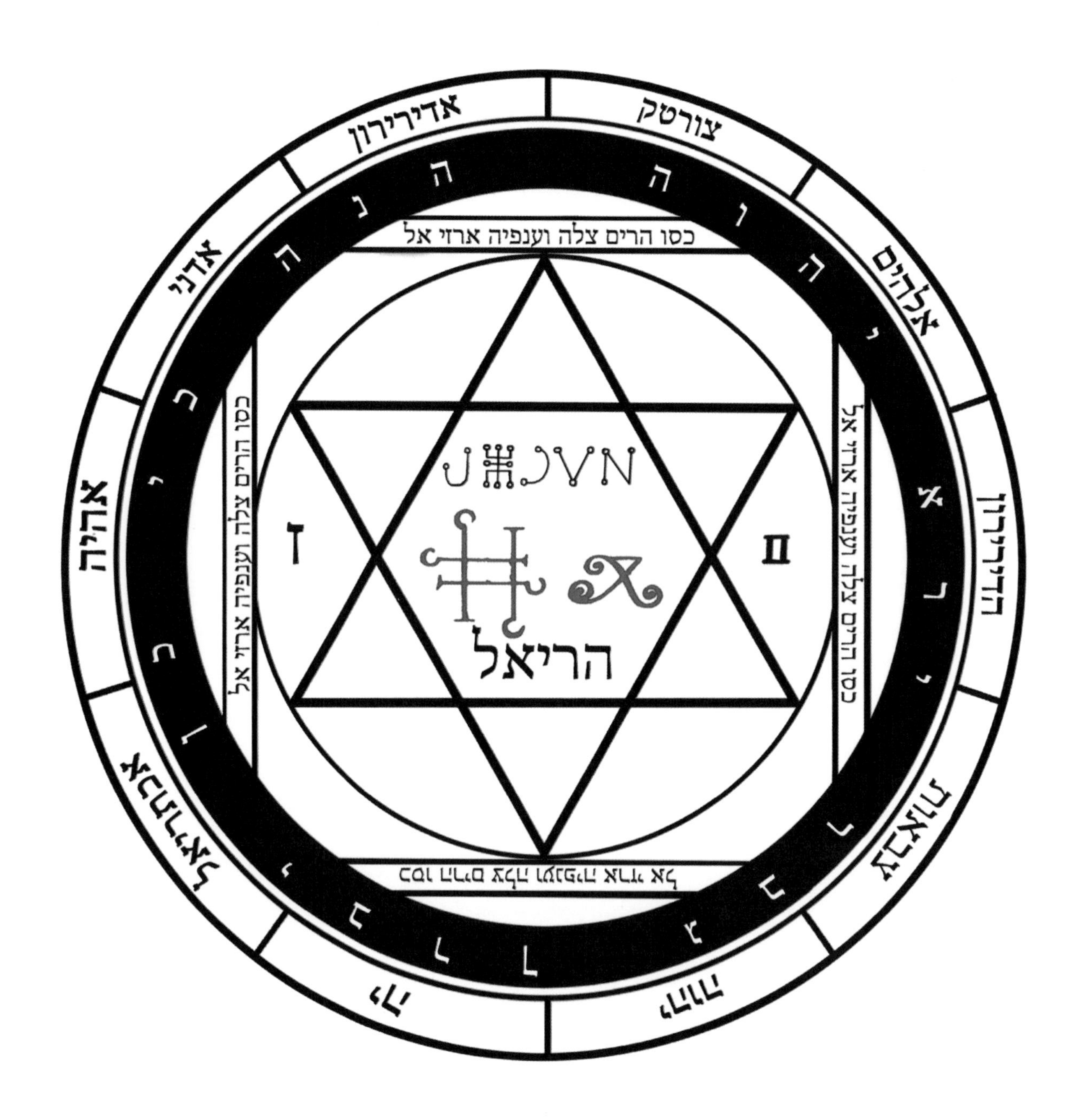

Hariel

HAH-REE-ELL

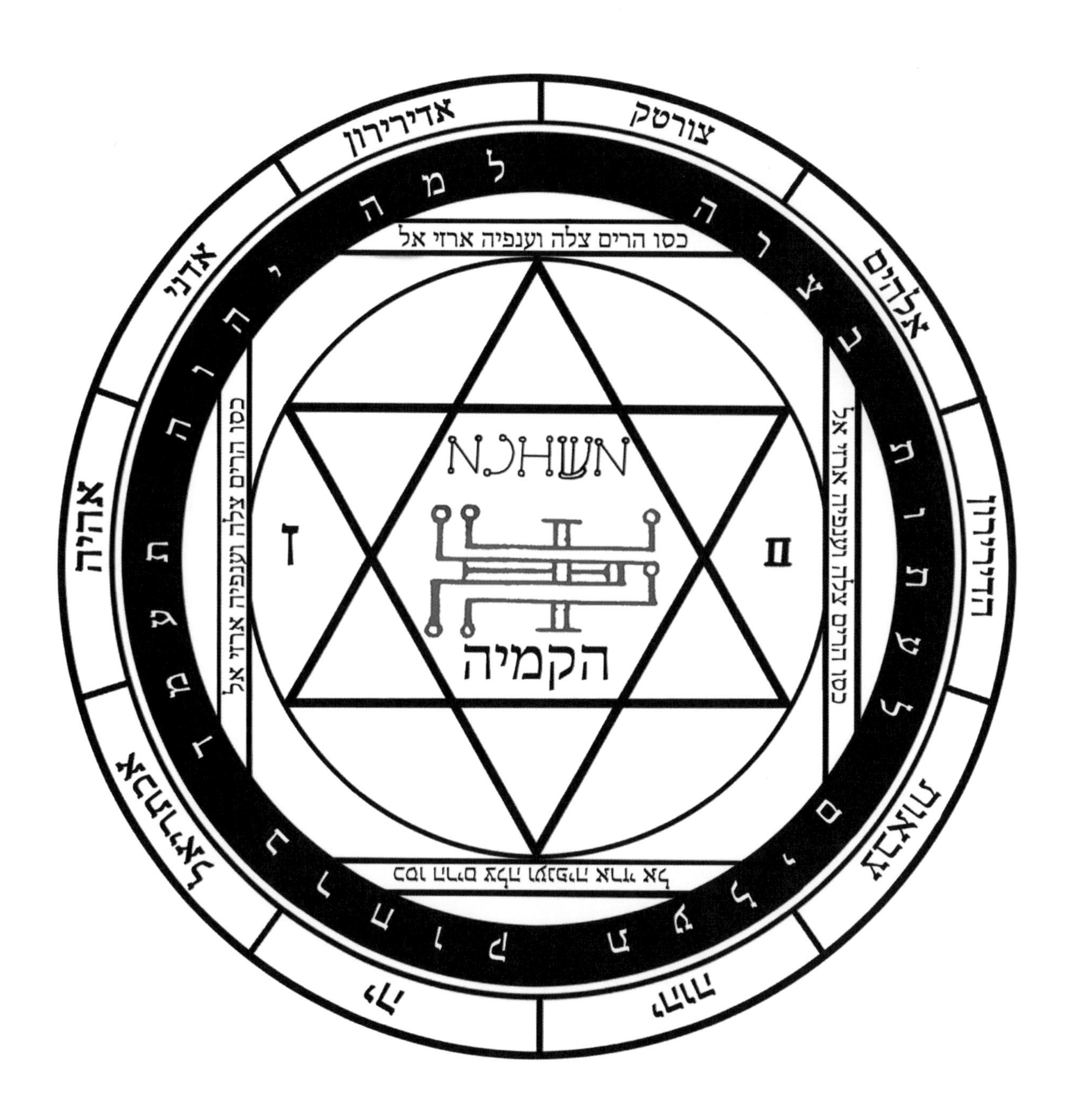

Hakemiah

HAH-KEM-EE-AH

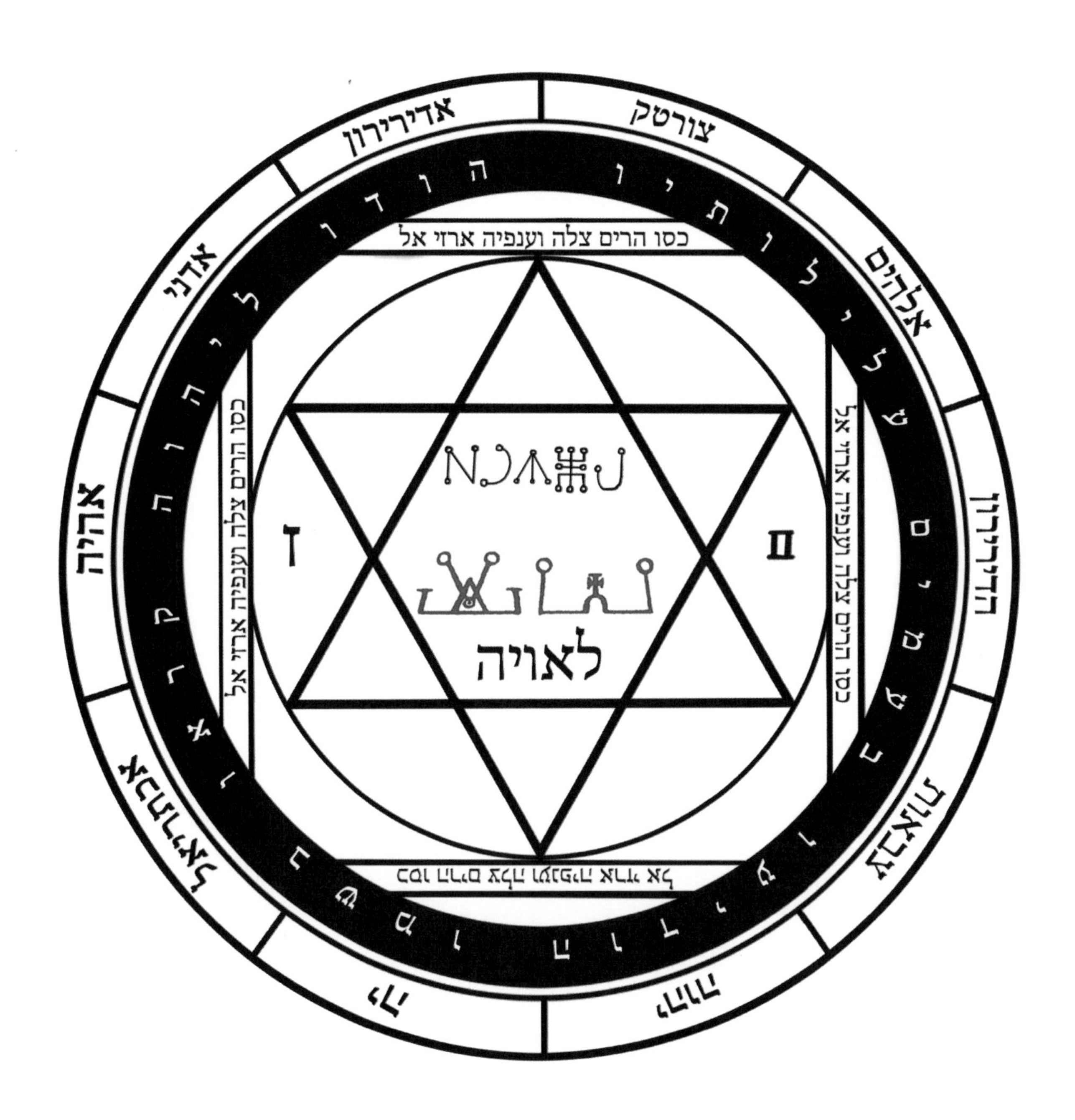

Lavel

LAH-VELL

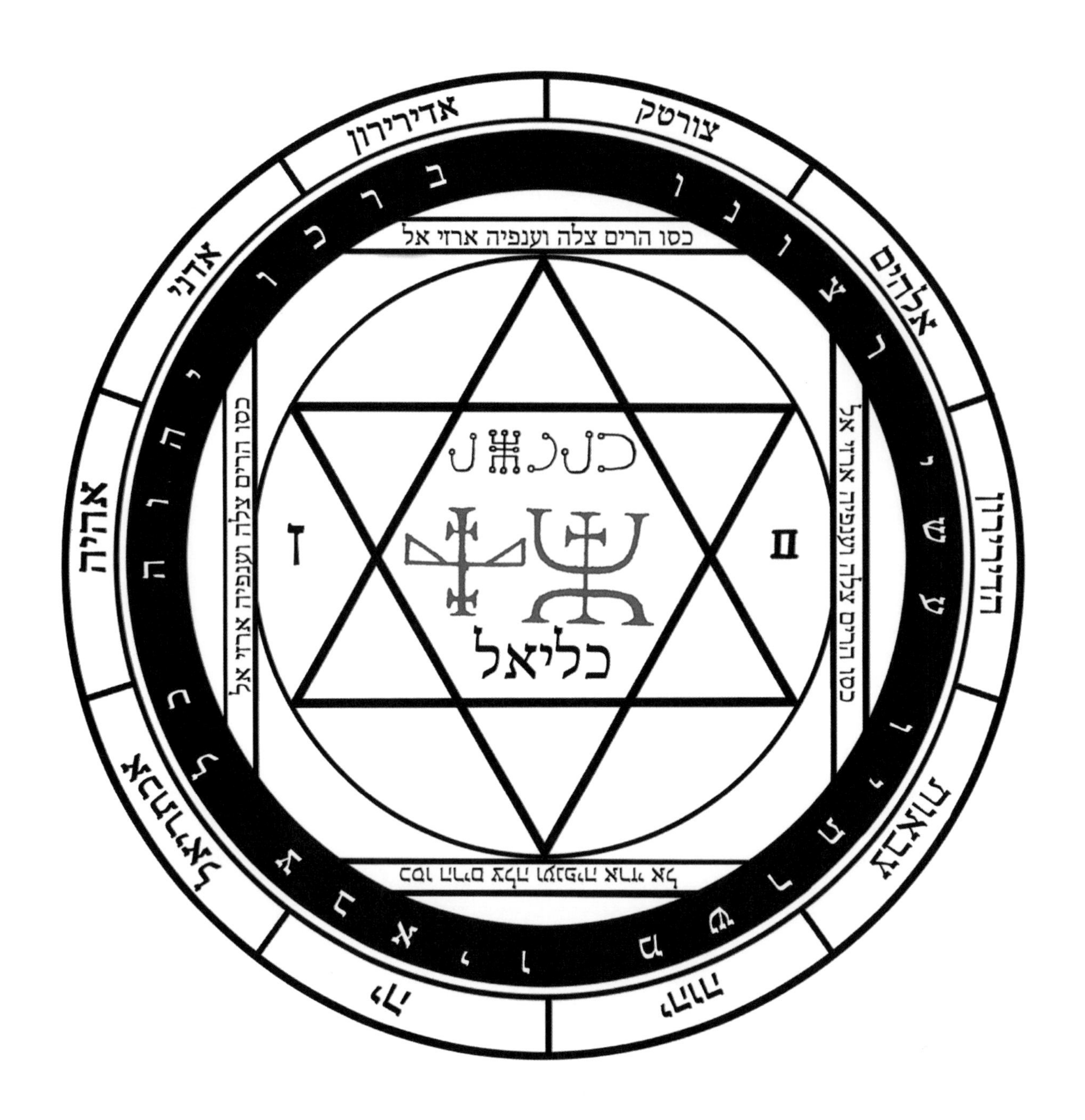

Keliel

KEH-LEE-ELL

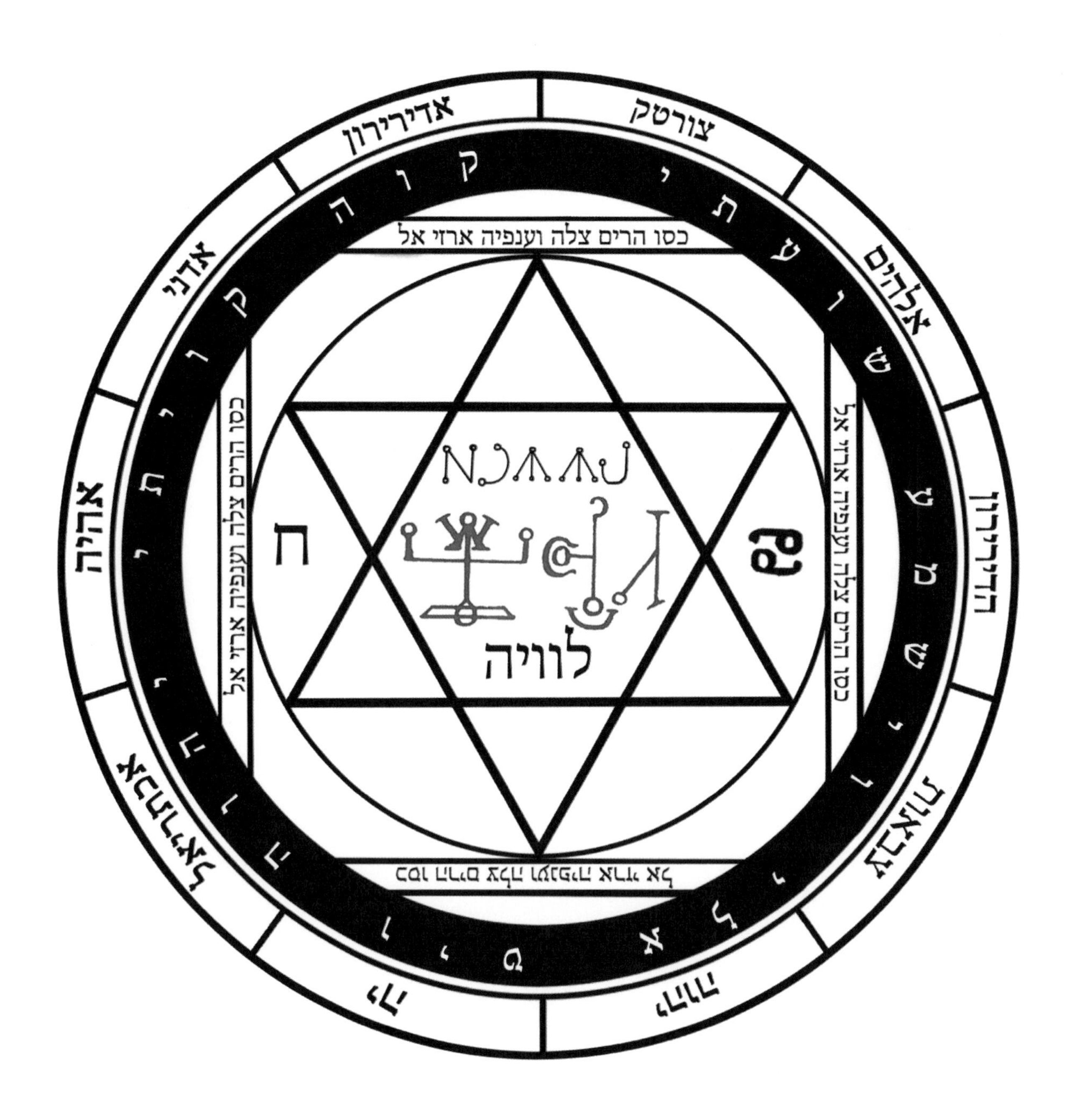

Lovel

LAW-VUH-ELL

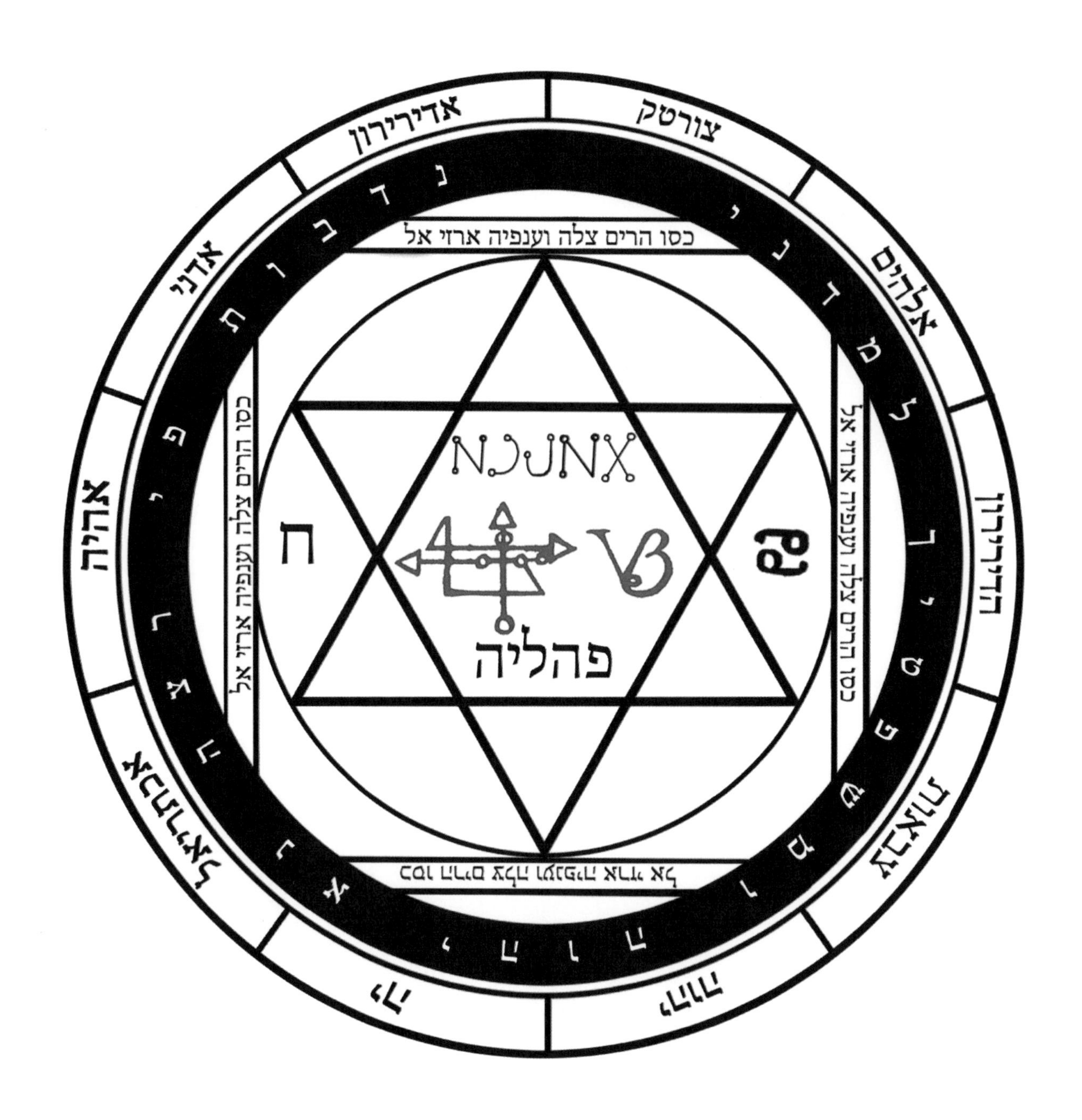

Pahaliah

PAH-HAH-LEE-AH

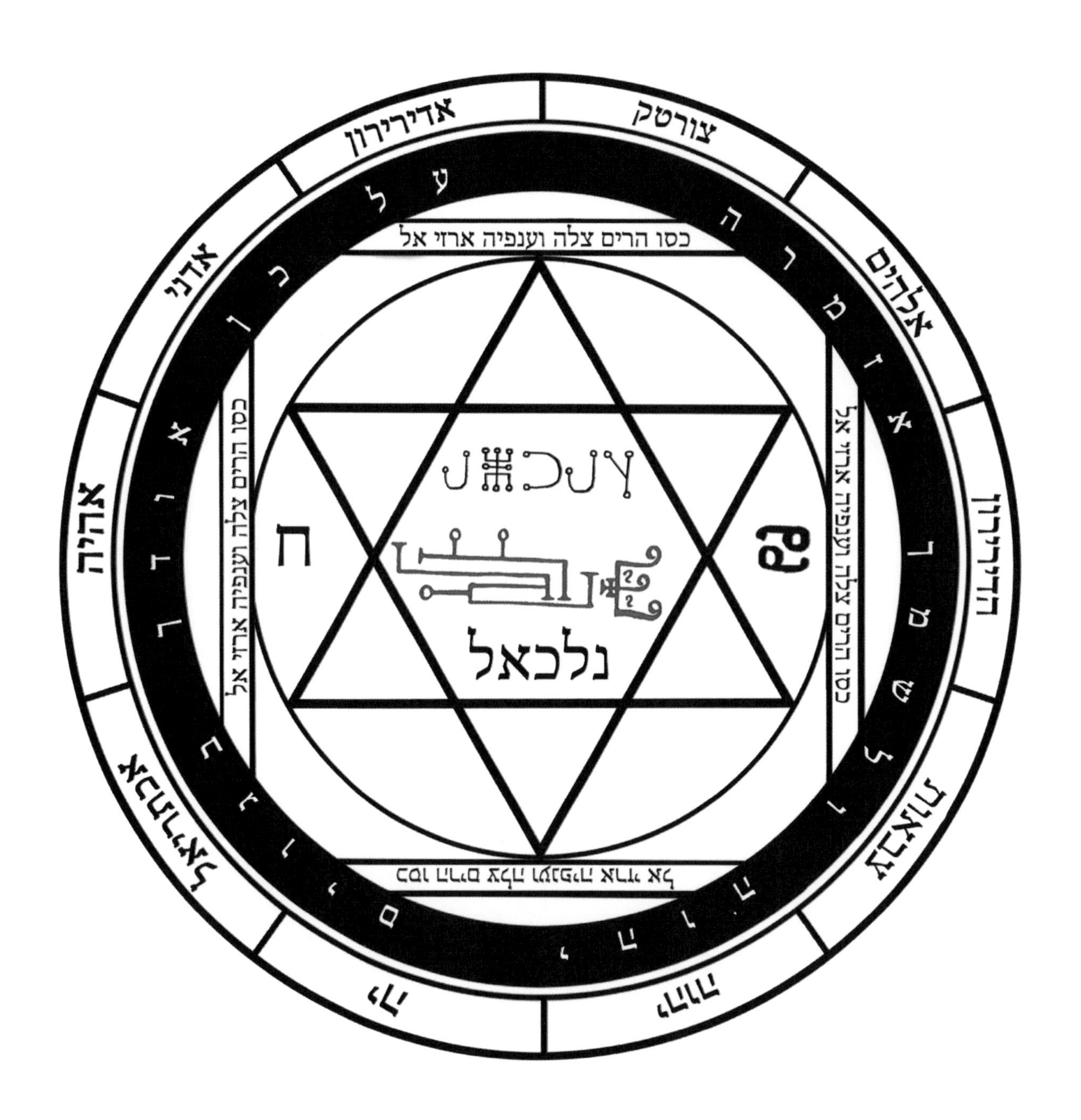

Nelachael

NELL-AH-CHELL

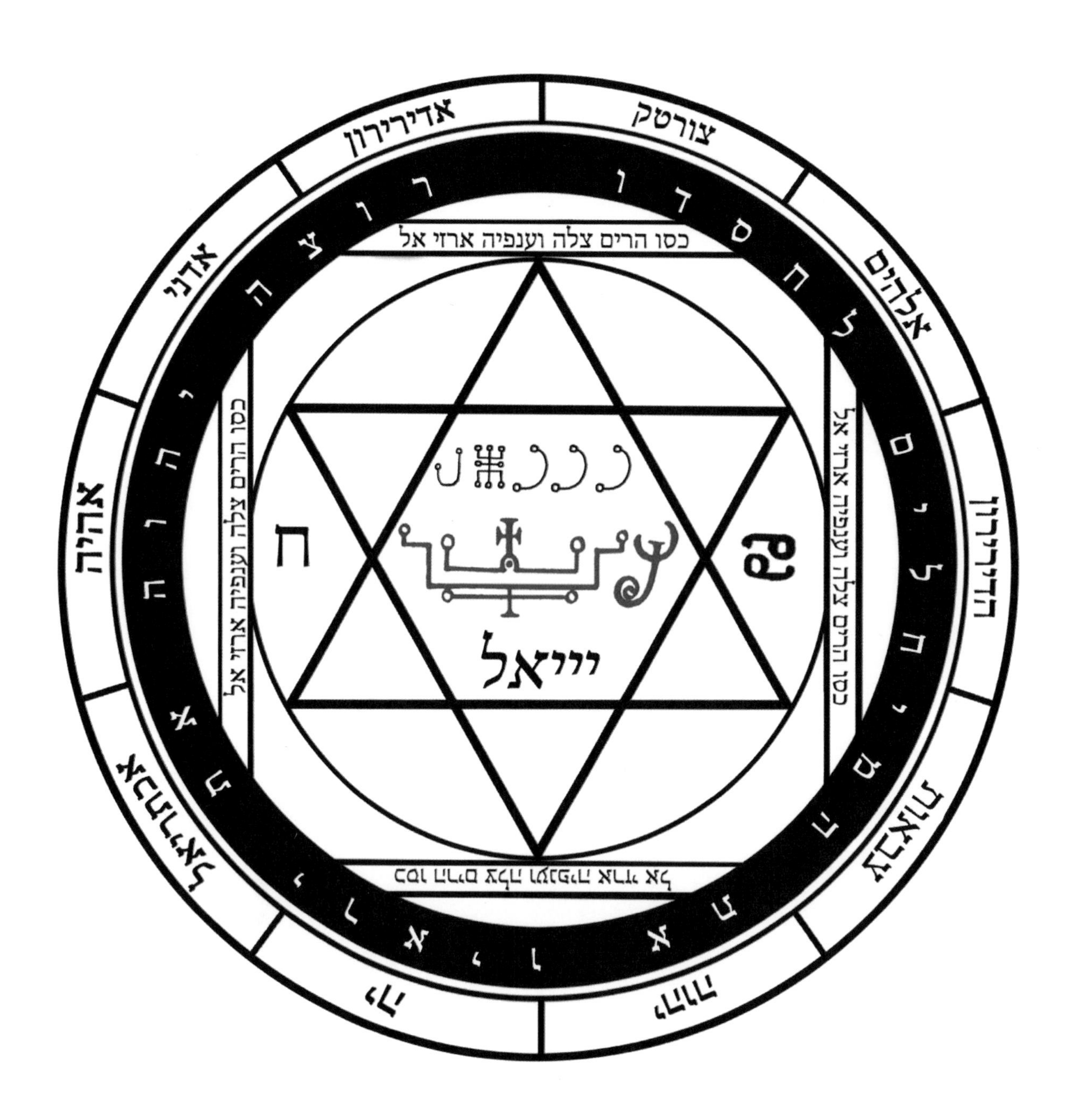

Yeyayel

YEH-YAH-EE-ELL

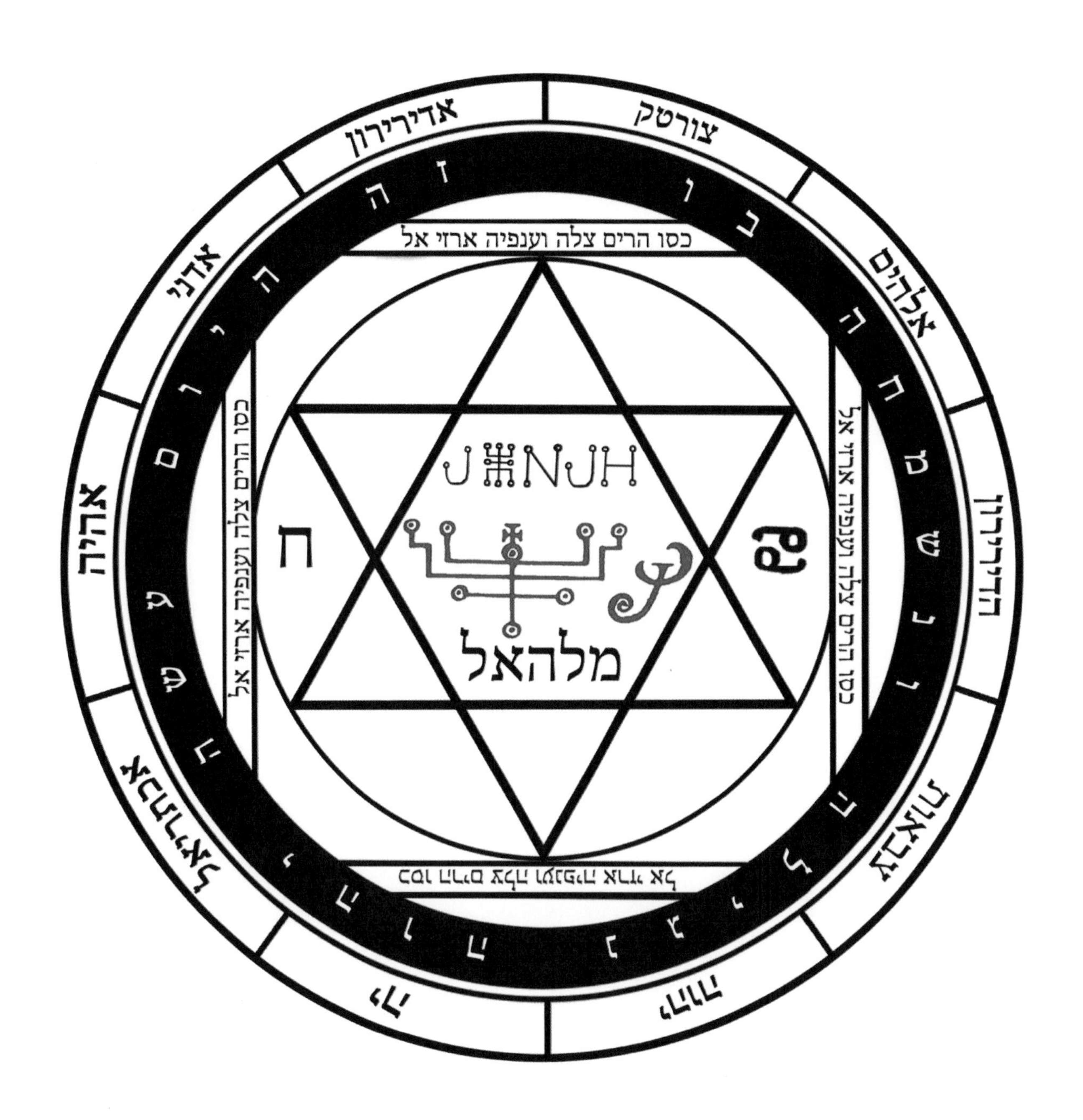

Melahel

MEH-LAH-ELL

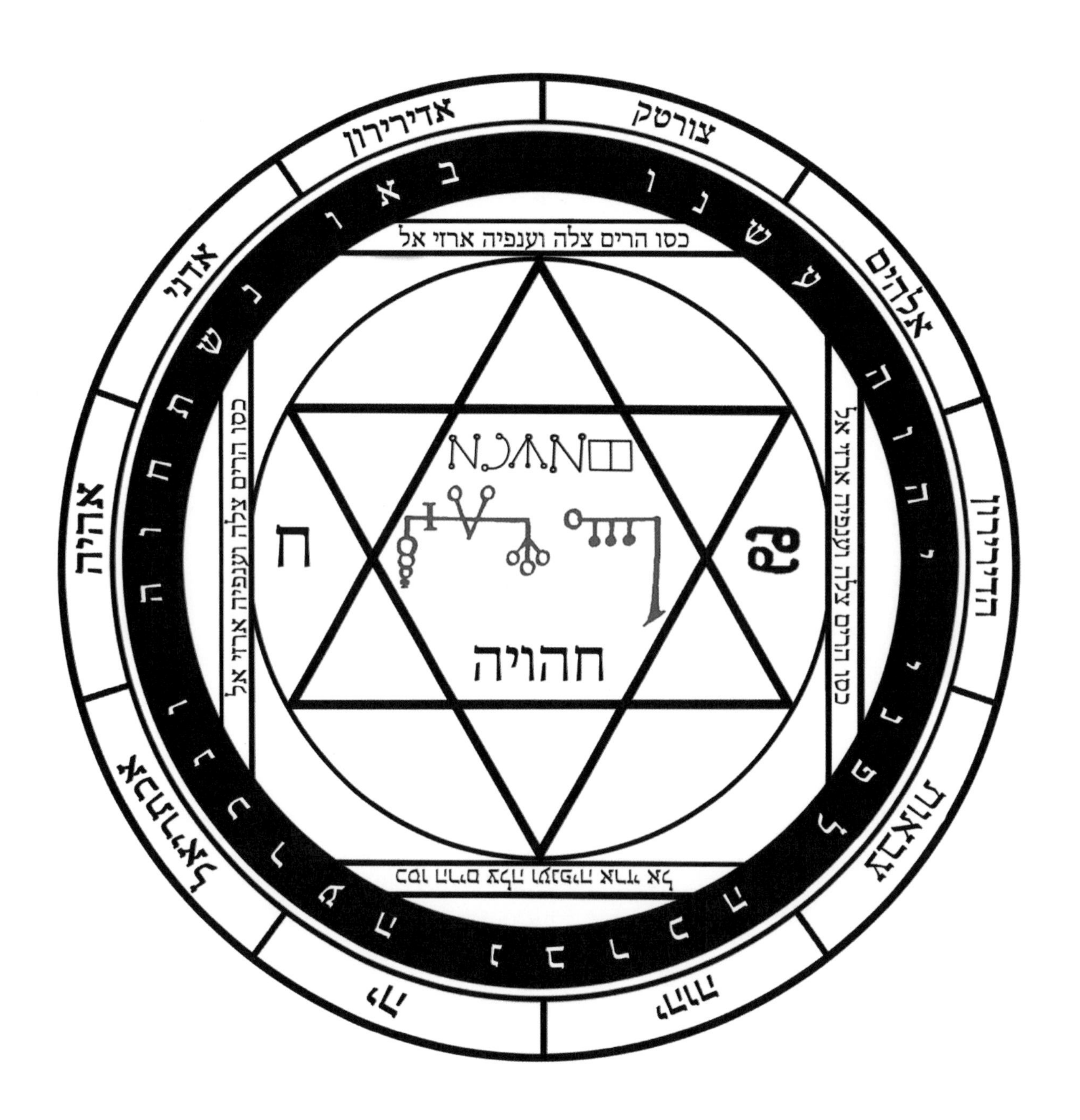

Chahuiah

CHAH-WHO-EE-AH

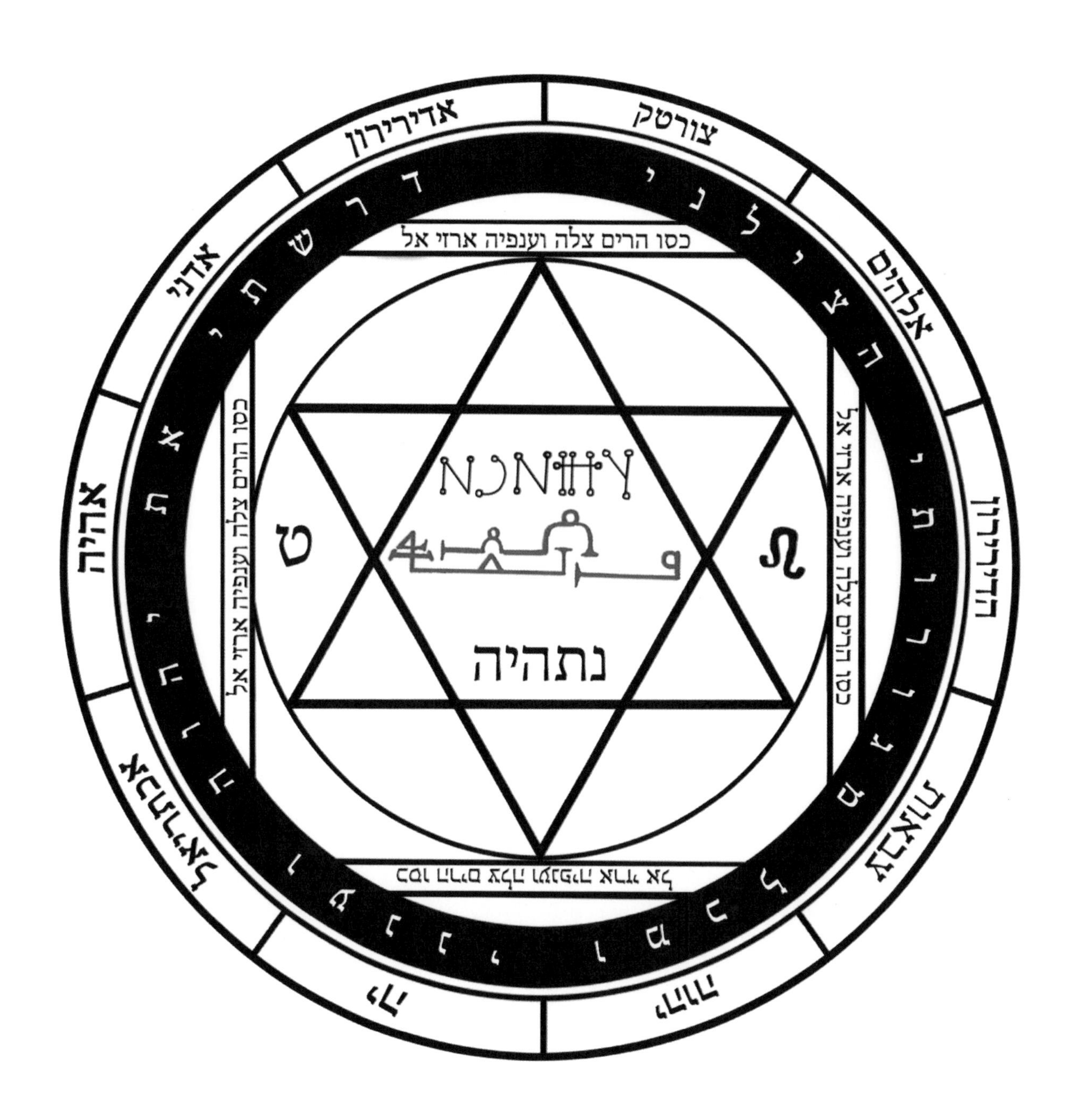

Netahiah

NET-AH-EE-YA

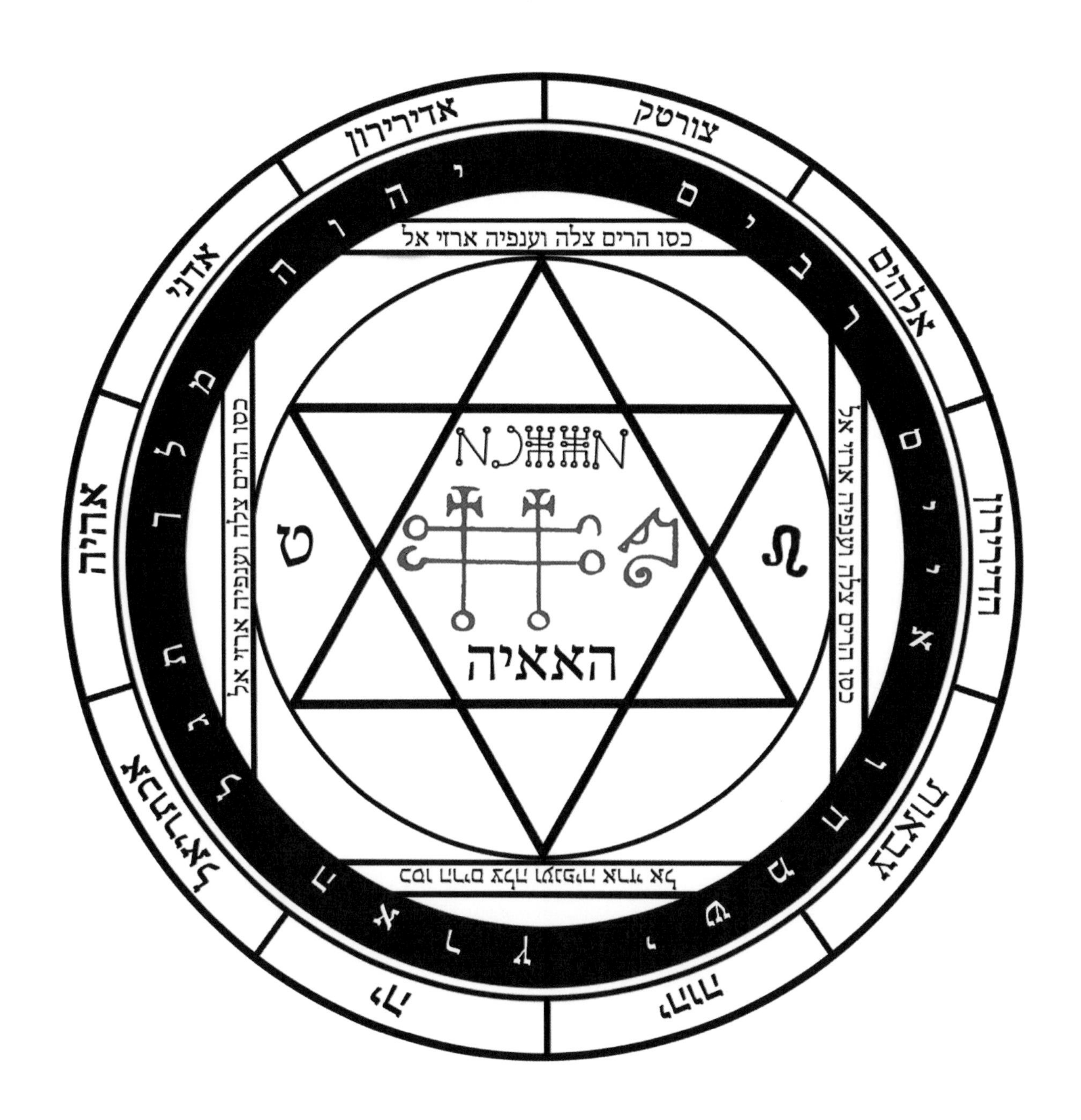

Haaiah

HAH-AH-EE-AH

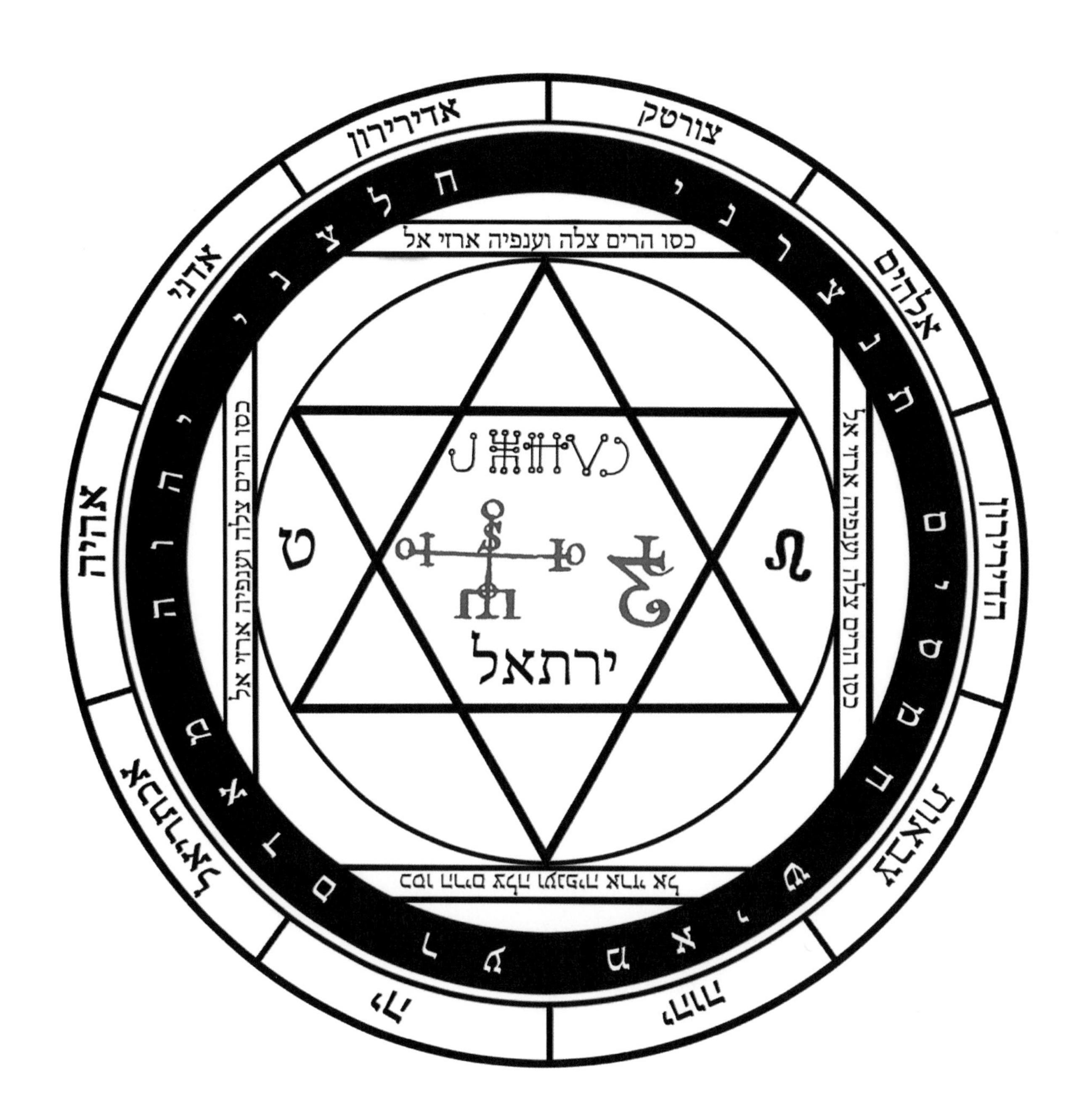

Yeretel

YEH-REH-TELL

Shahahiah

SHAH-AH-EE-AH

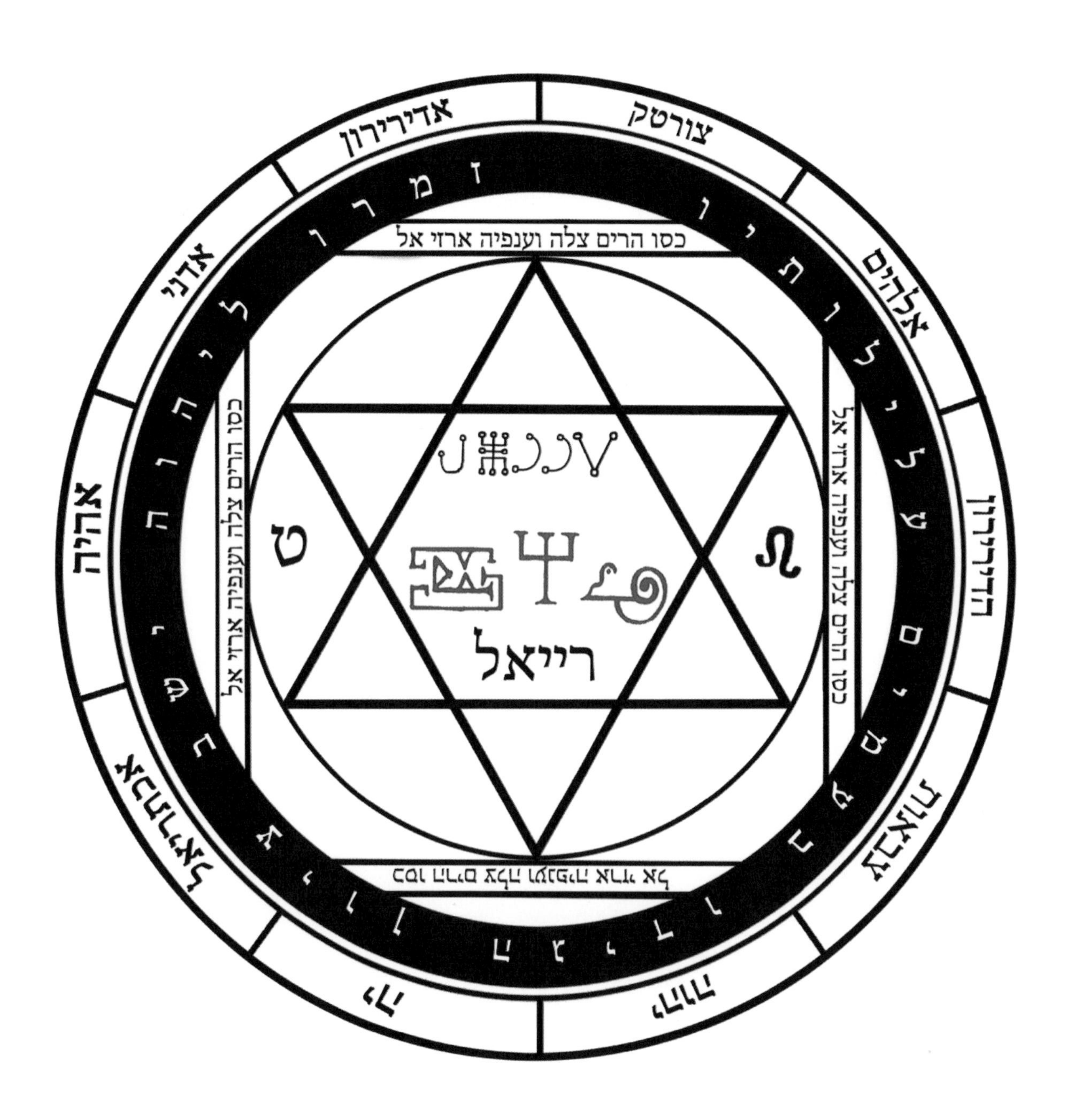

Riyiyel

REE-EE-ELL

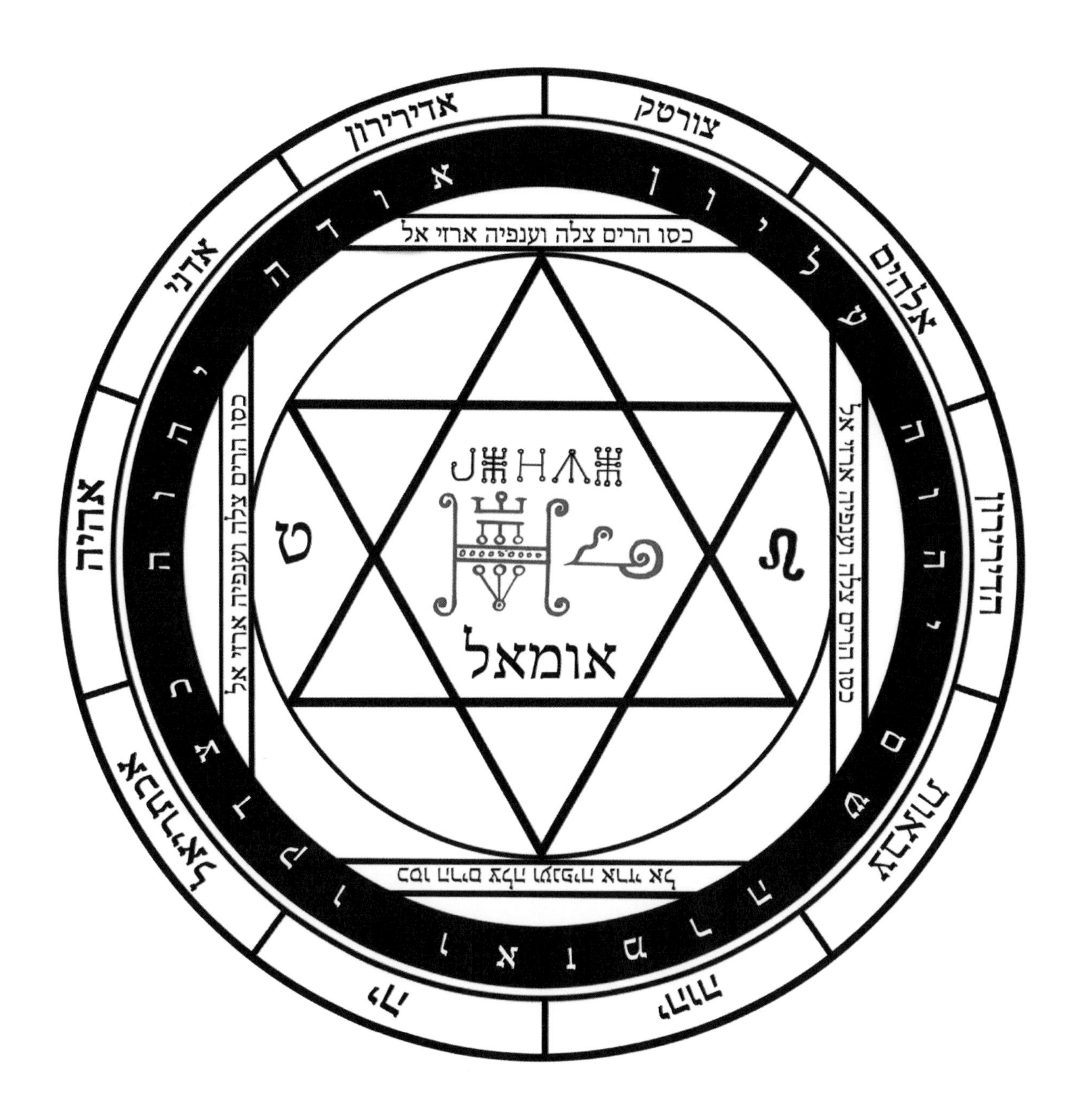

Omael

AWE-MUH-ELL

Lecavel

LEK-AH-VELL

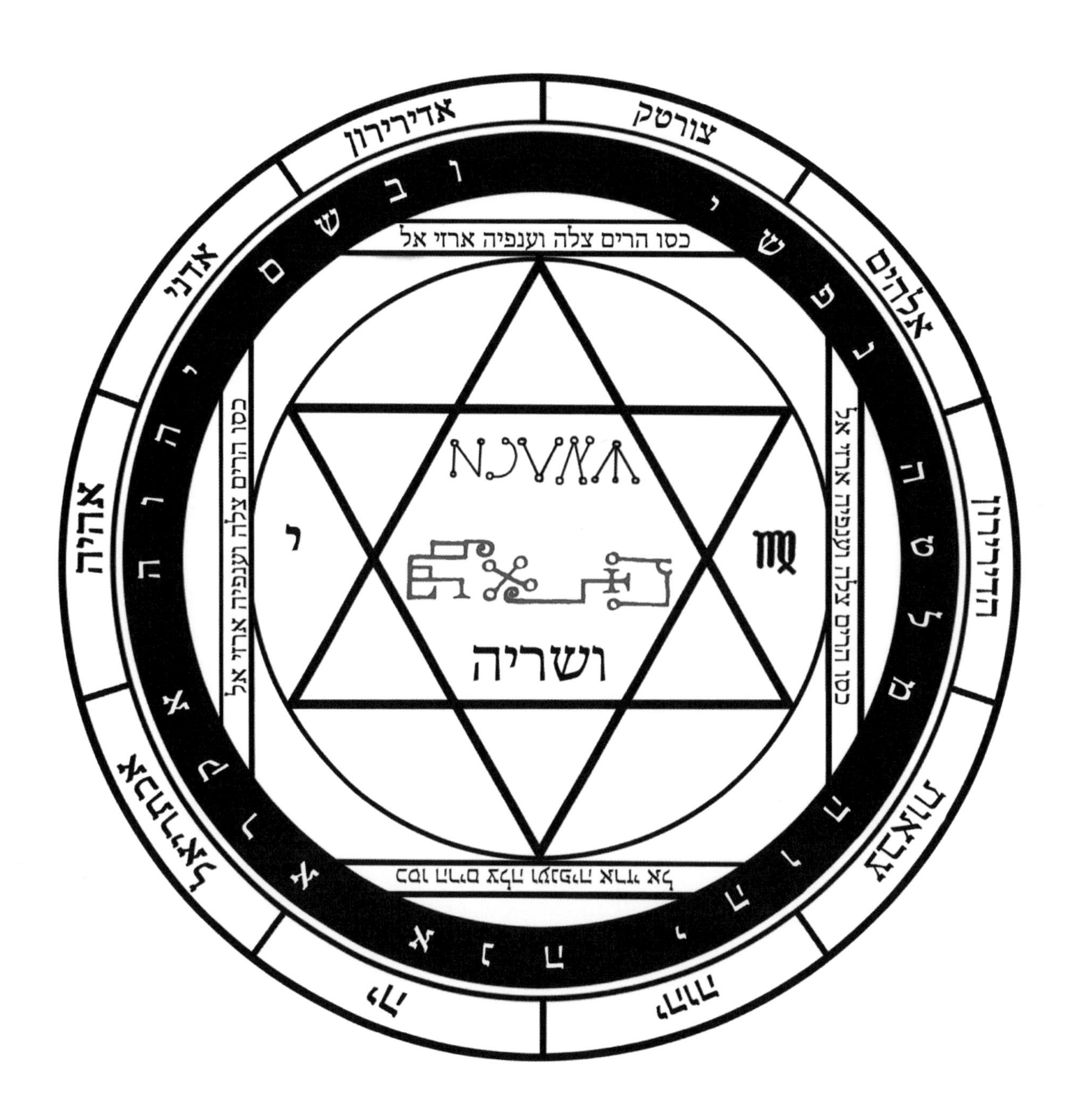

Vesheriah

VESH-EH-REE-AH

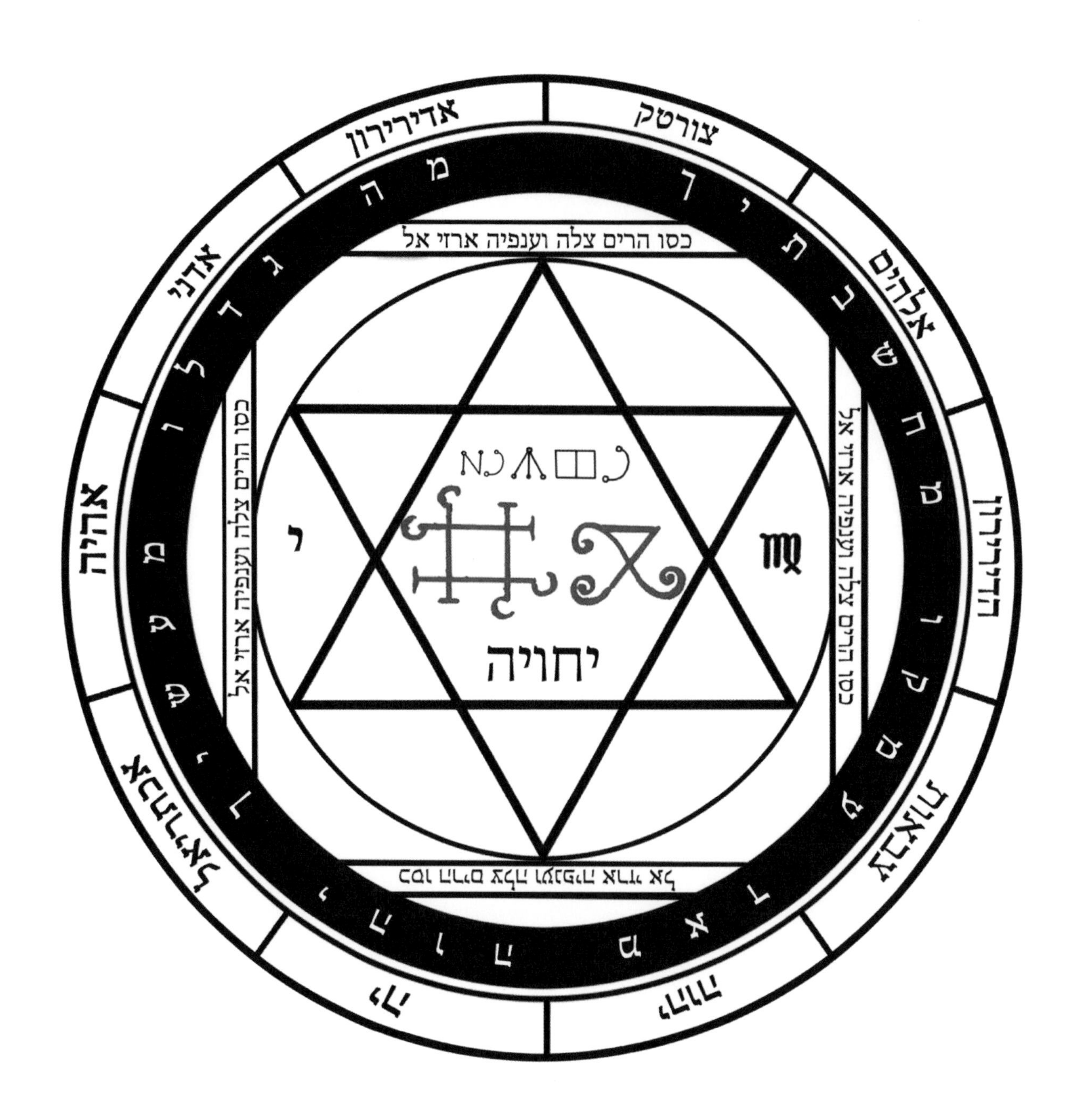

Yichuiah

YEE-CHOO-EE-AH

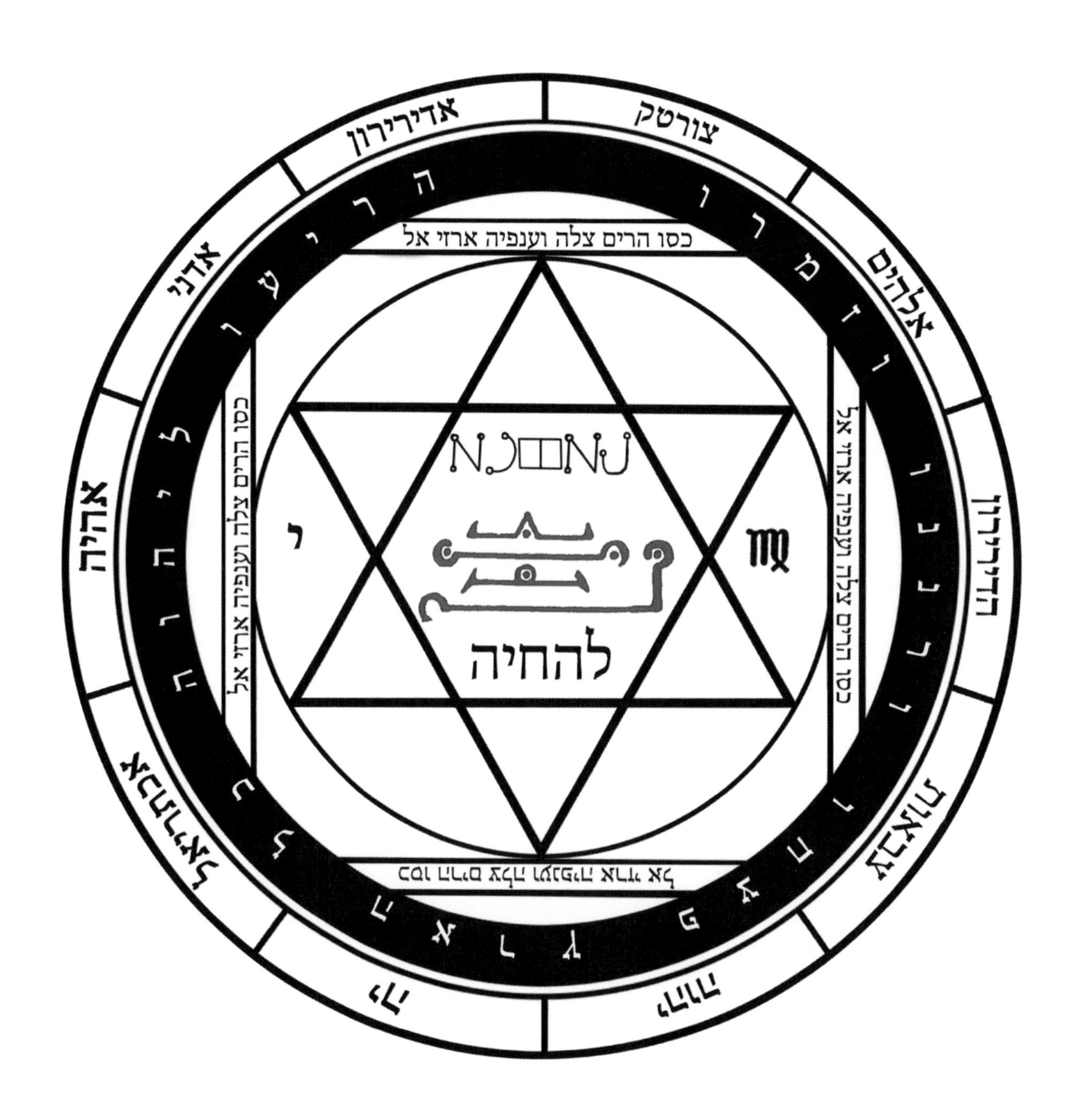

Lehachiah

LEH-HAH-CHEE-AH

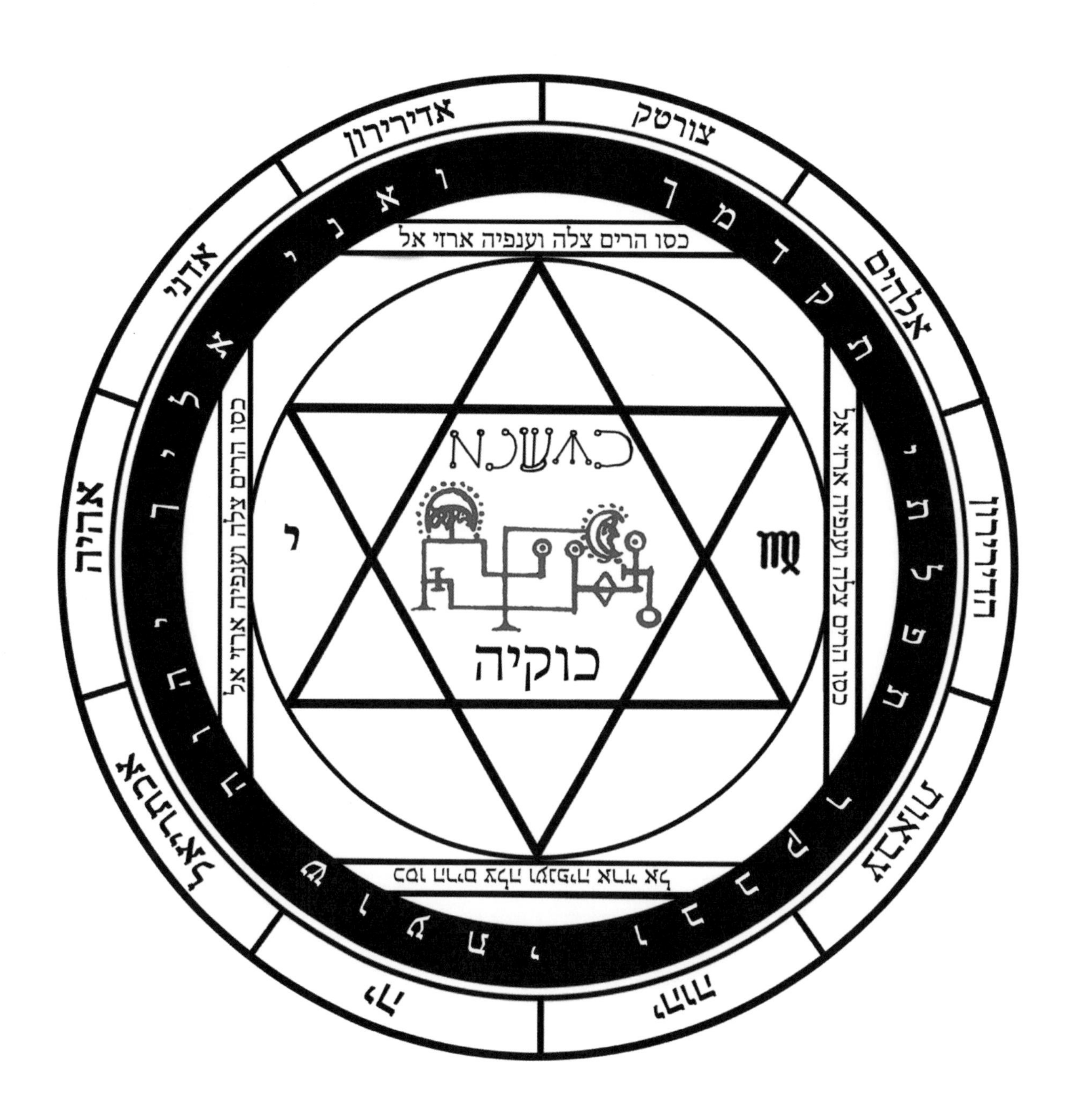

Kevekiah

KEV-EK-EE-AH

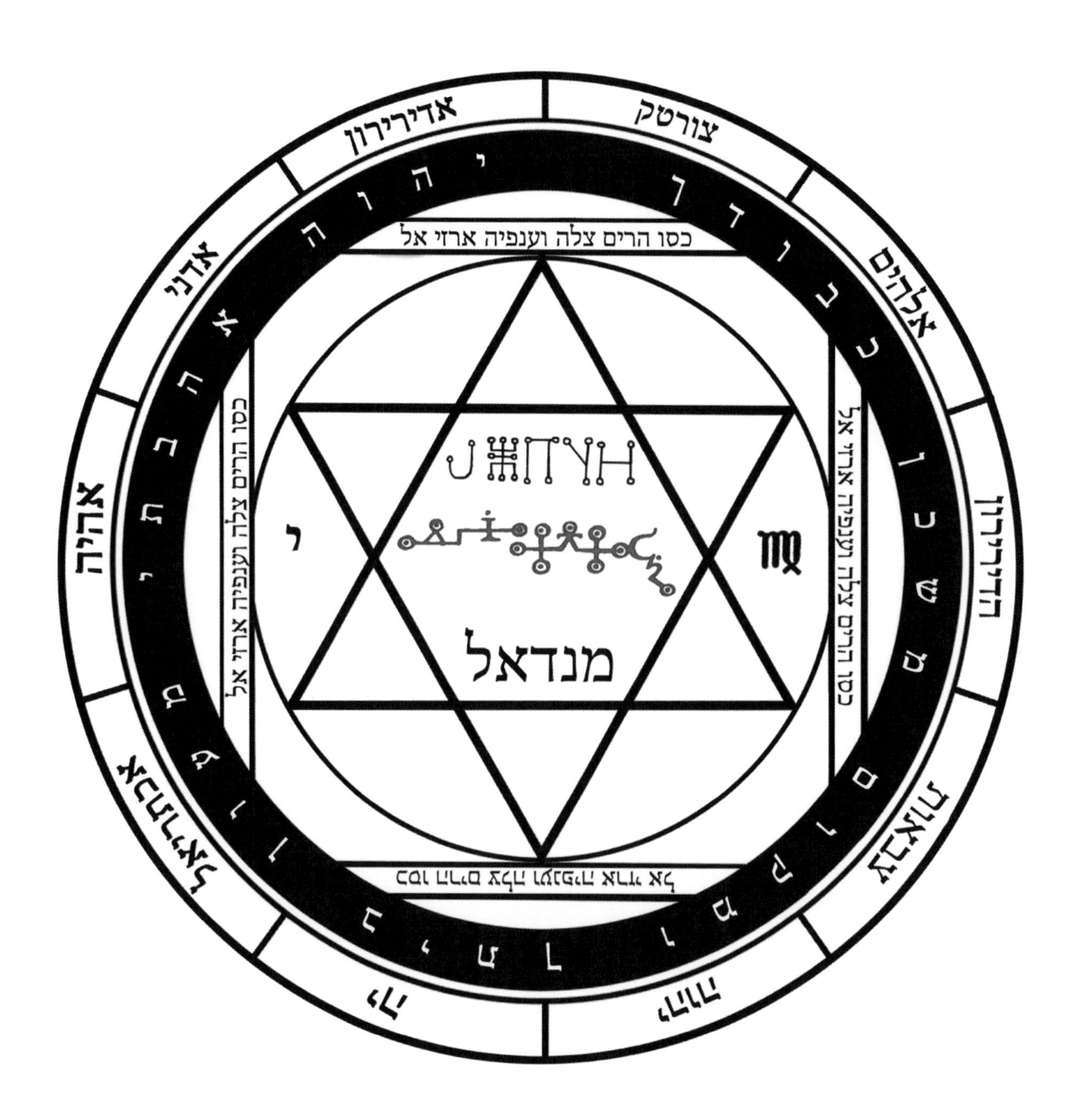

Menadel

MEN-AH-DELL

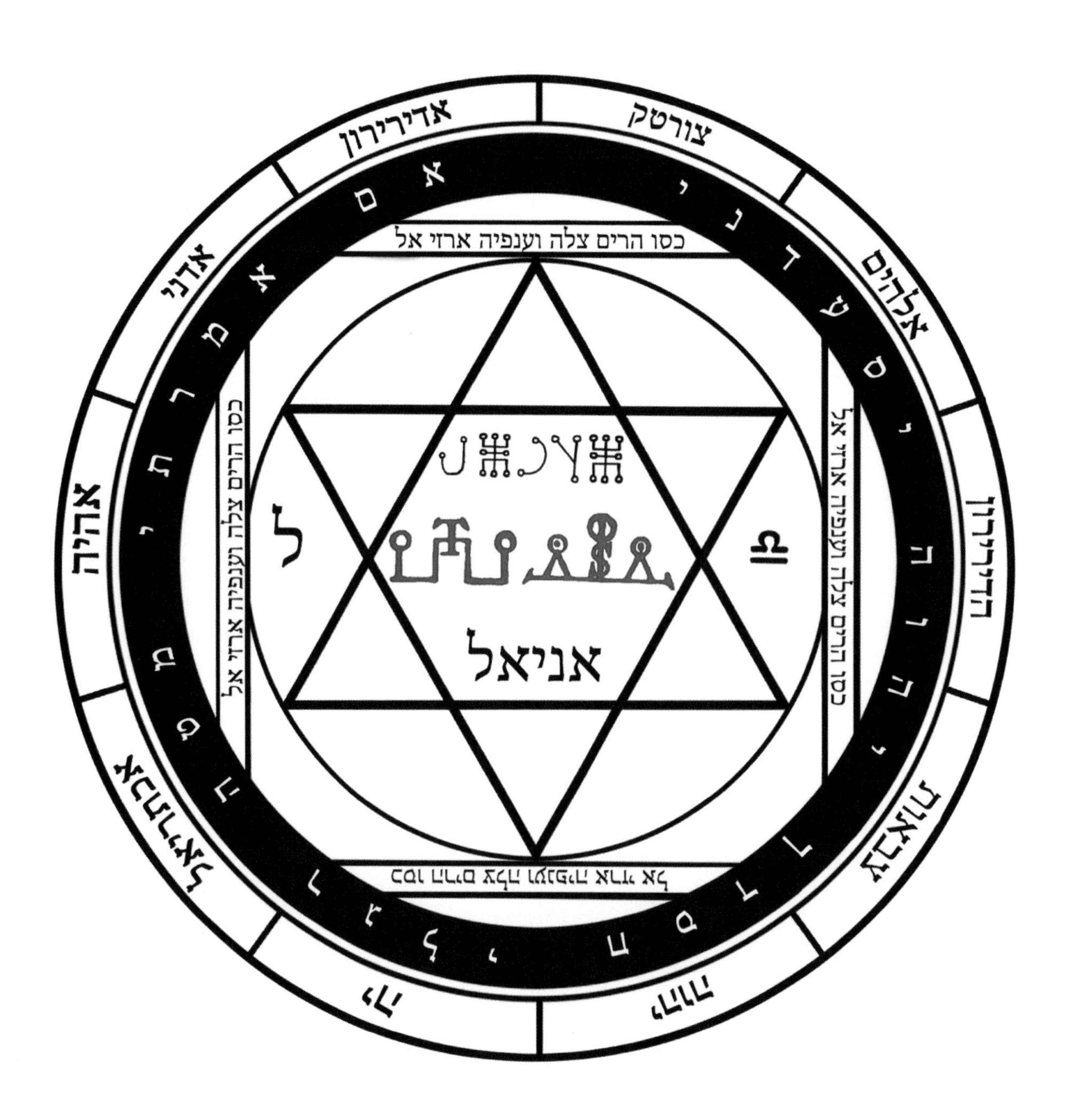

Aniel

AH-KNEE-ELL

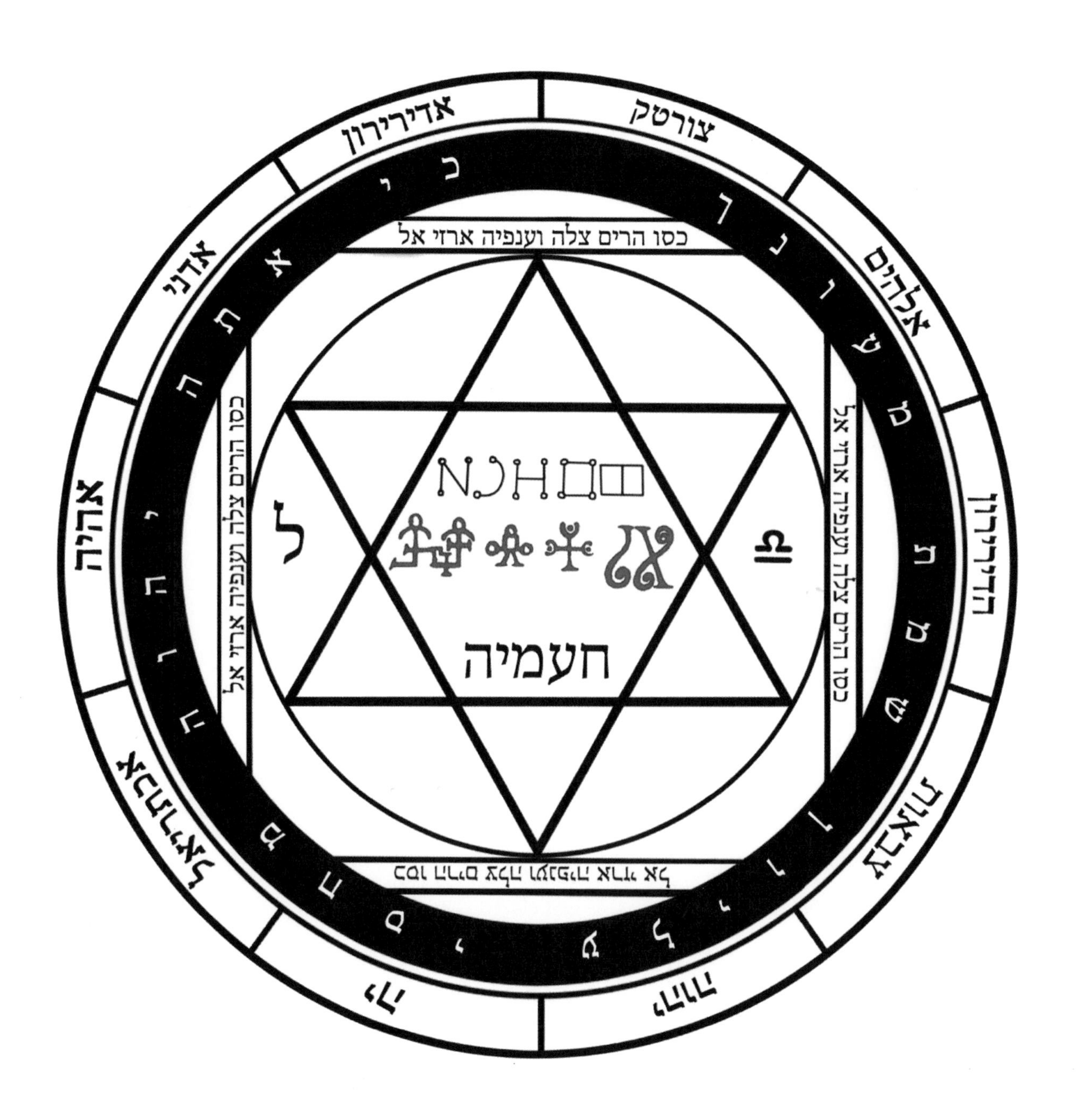

Chaamiah

CHAH-AH-ME-AH

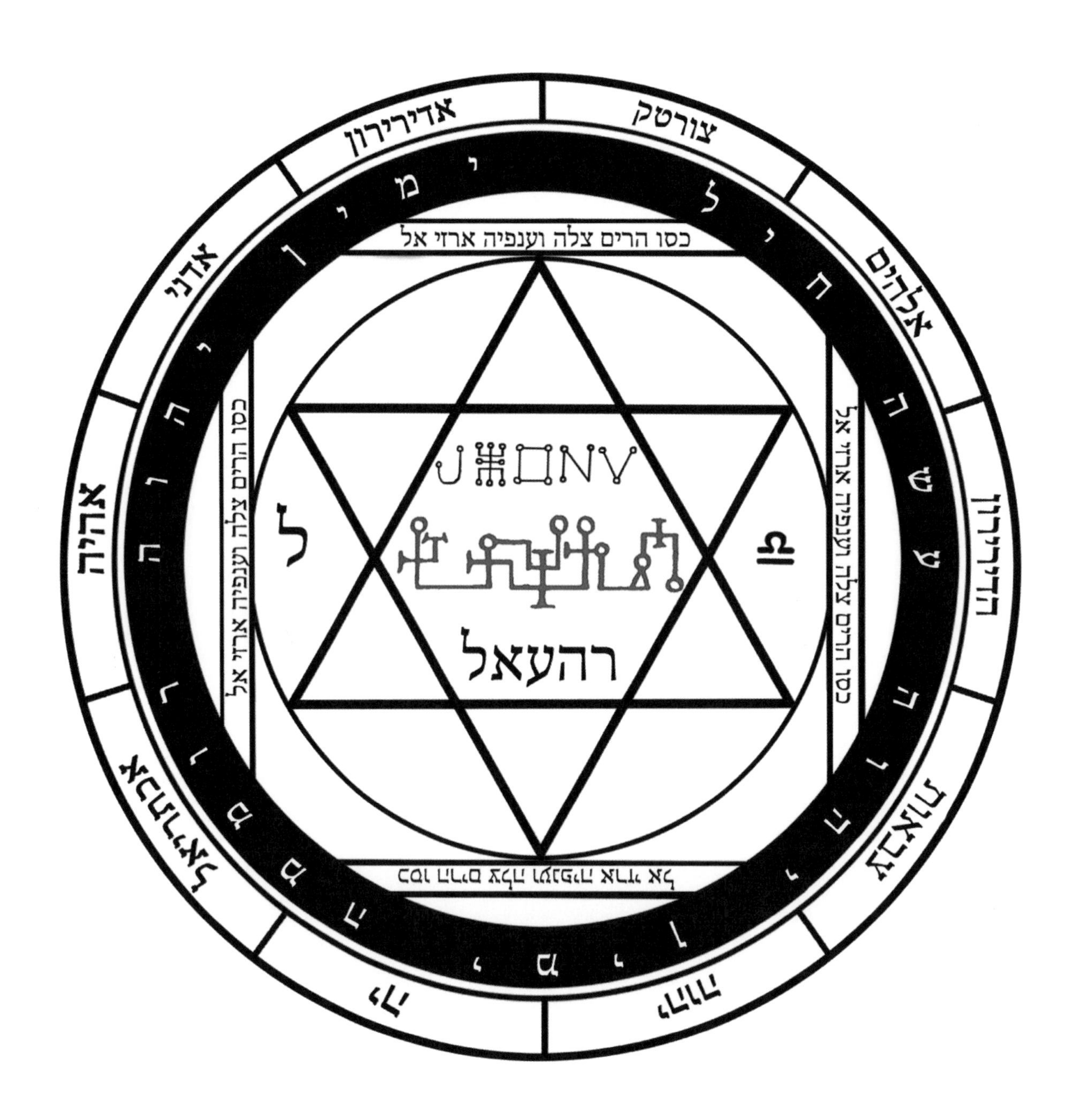

Rehoel

REH-HAW-ELL

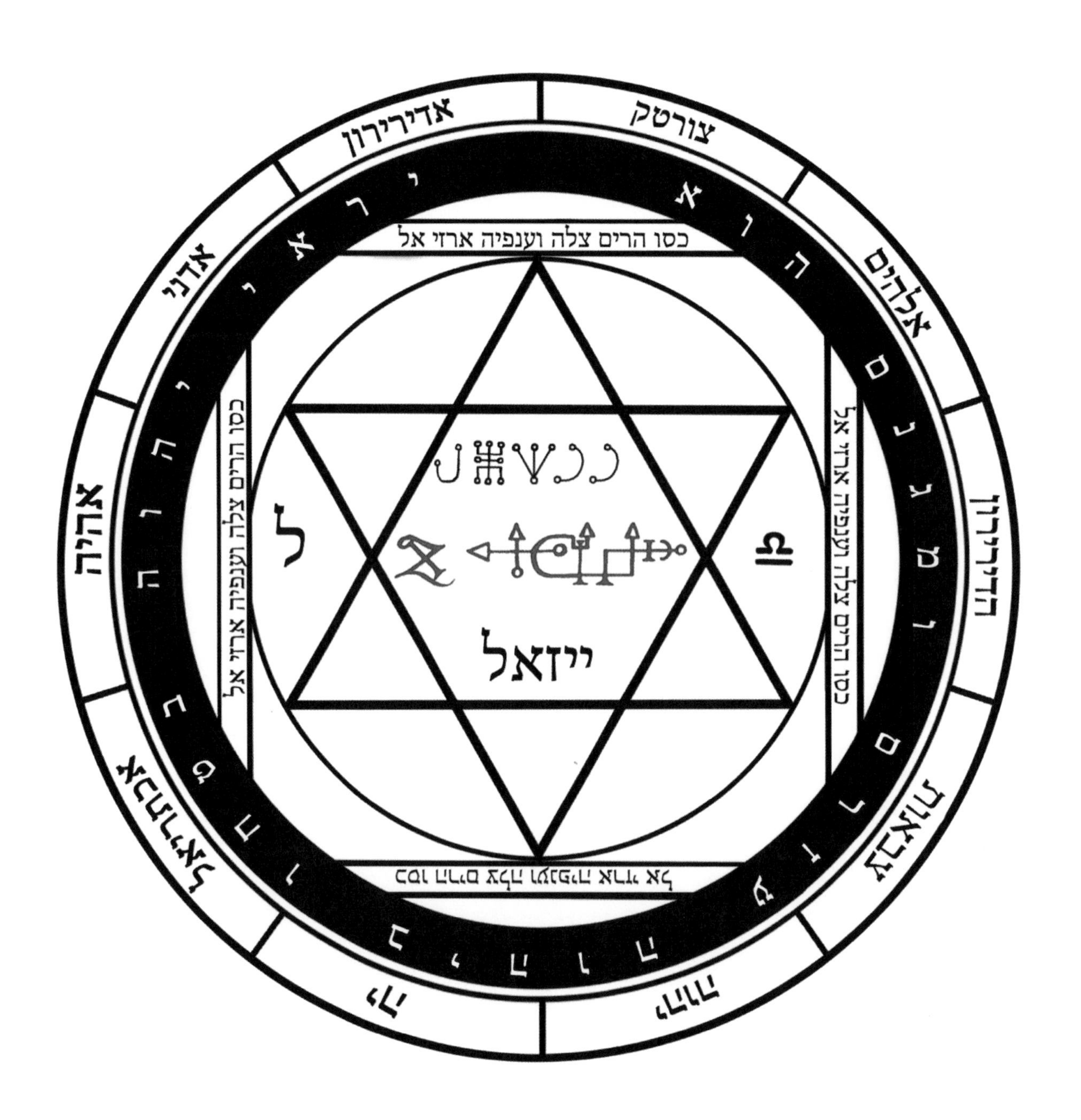

Yeyizel

YAY-EEZ-ELL

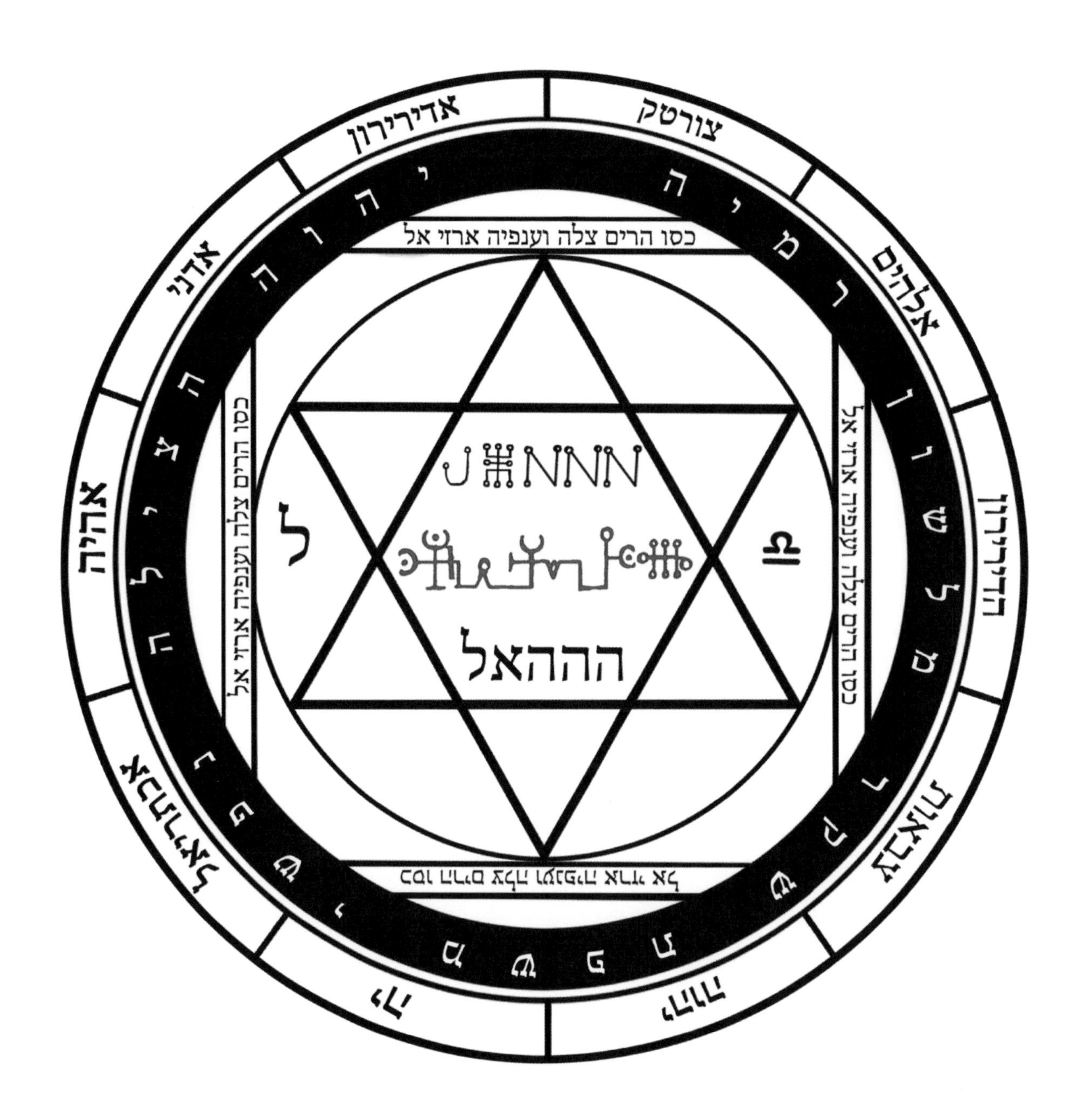

Hahahel

HAH-AH-ELL

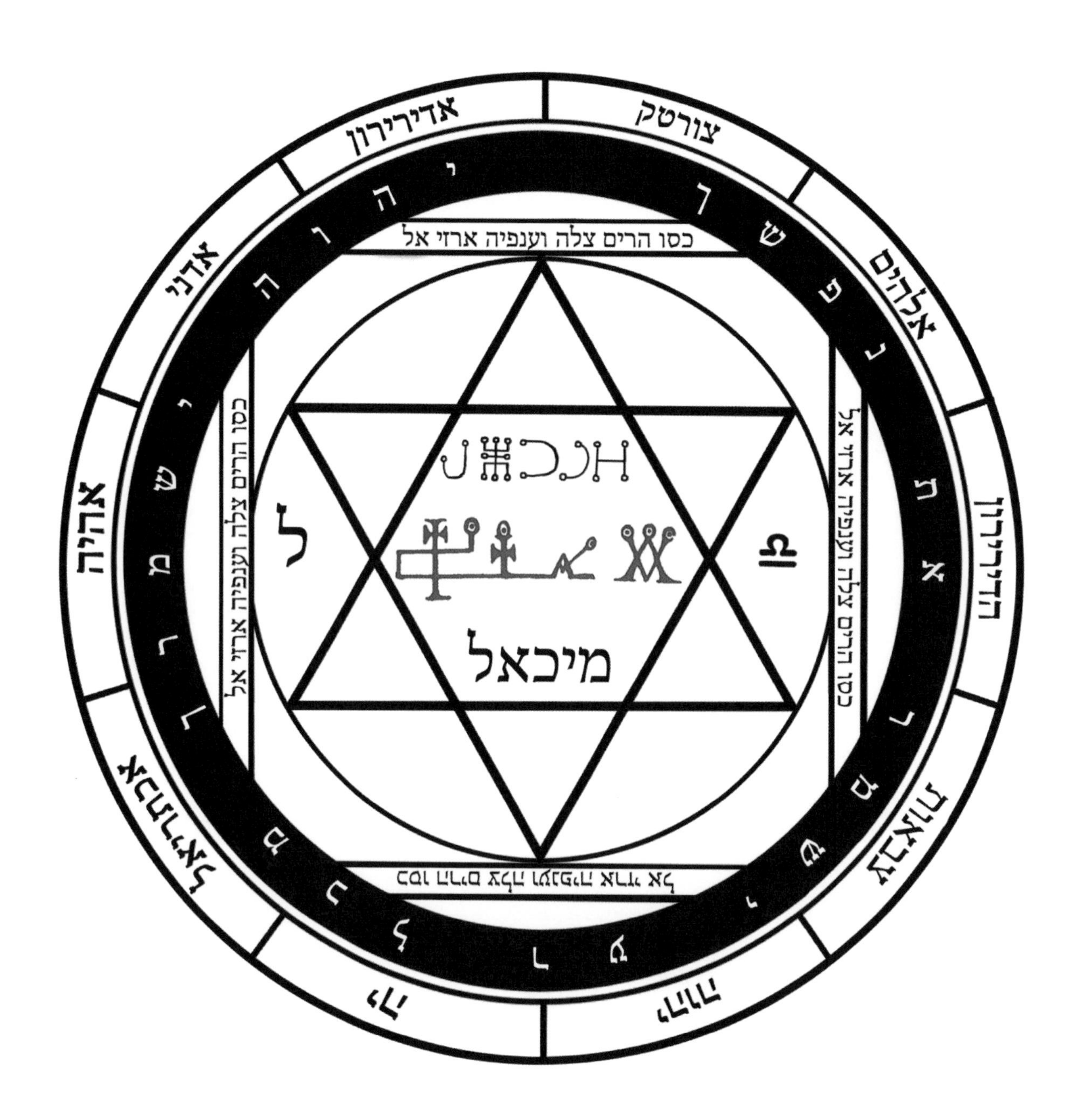

Michel

ME-CHUH-ELL

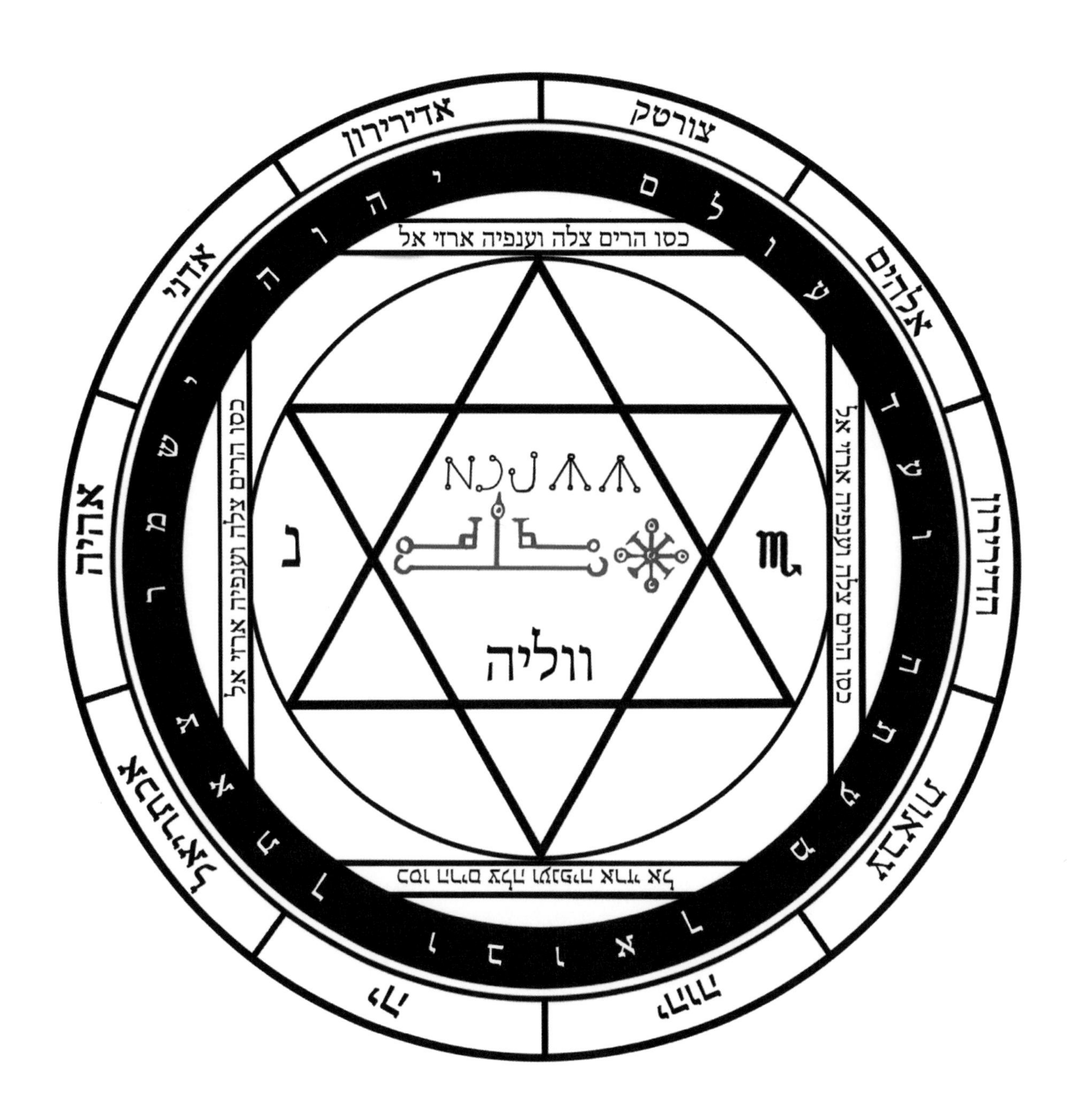

Vevaliah

VEH-VAH-LEE-AH

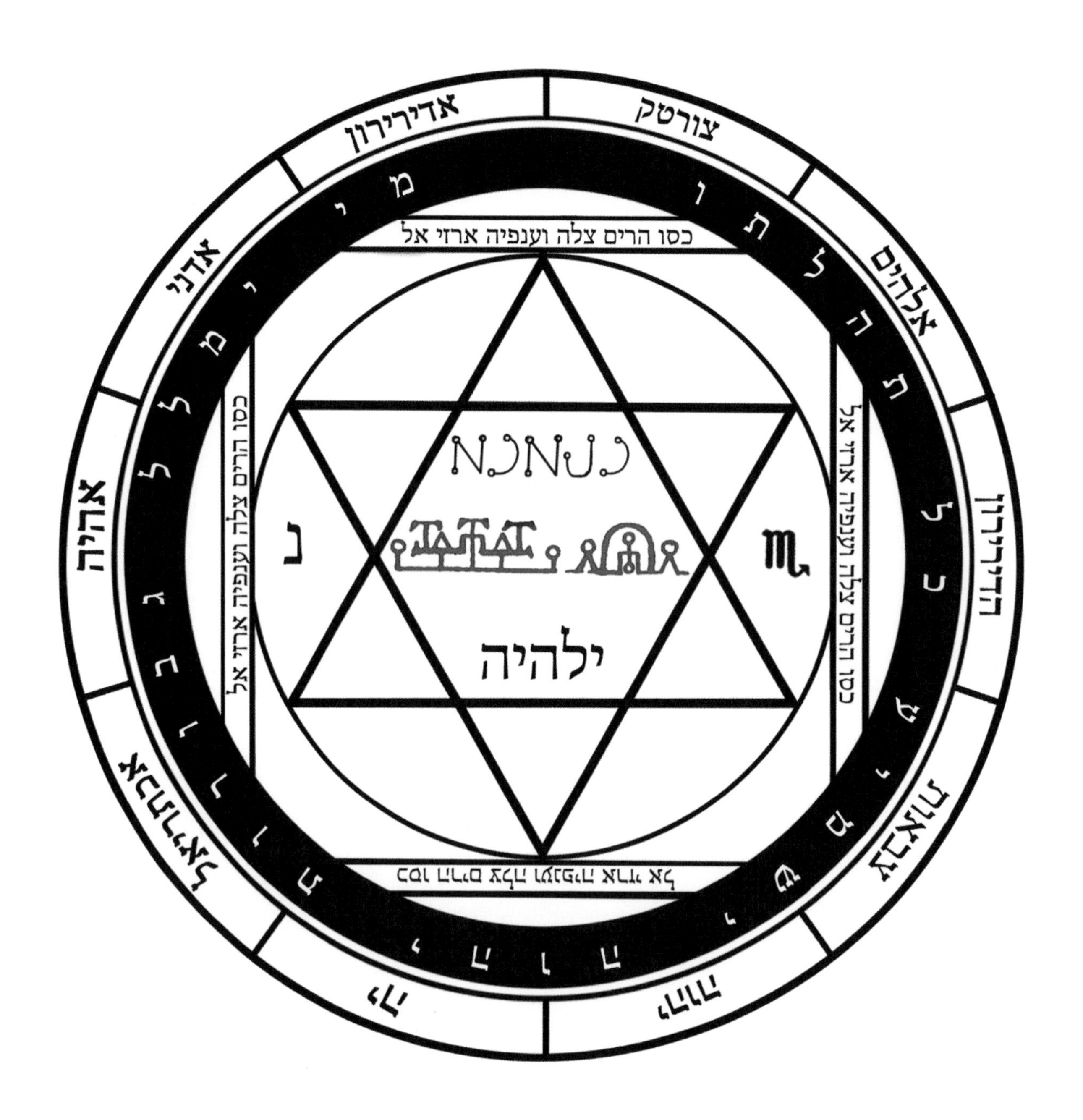

Yelahiah

YELL-AH-EE-AH

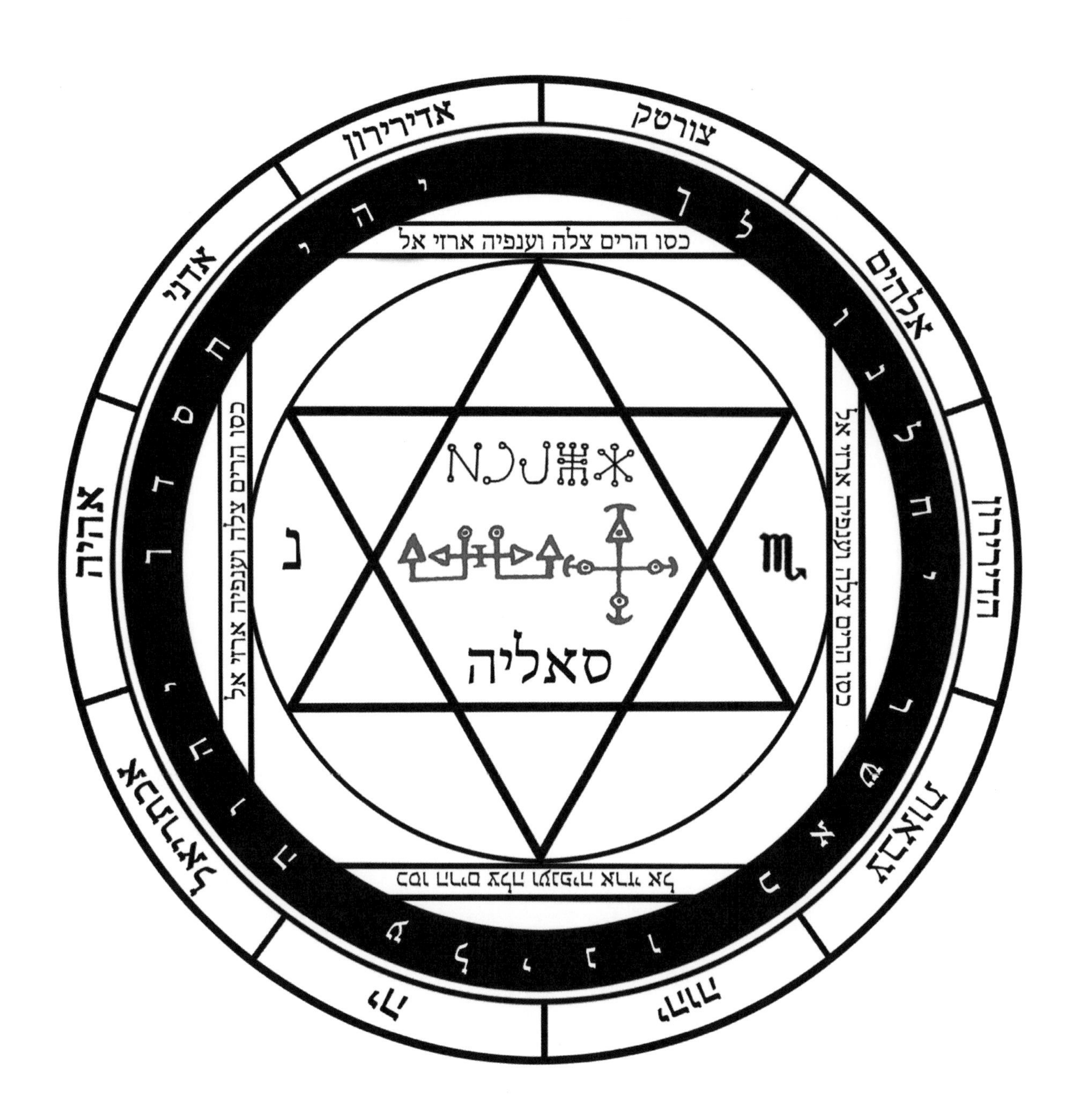

Sealiah

SEH-AH-LEE-AH

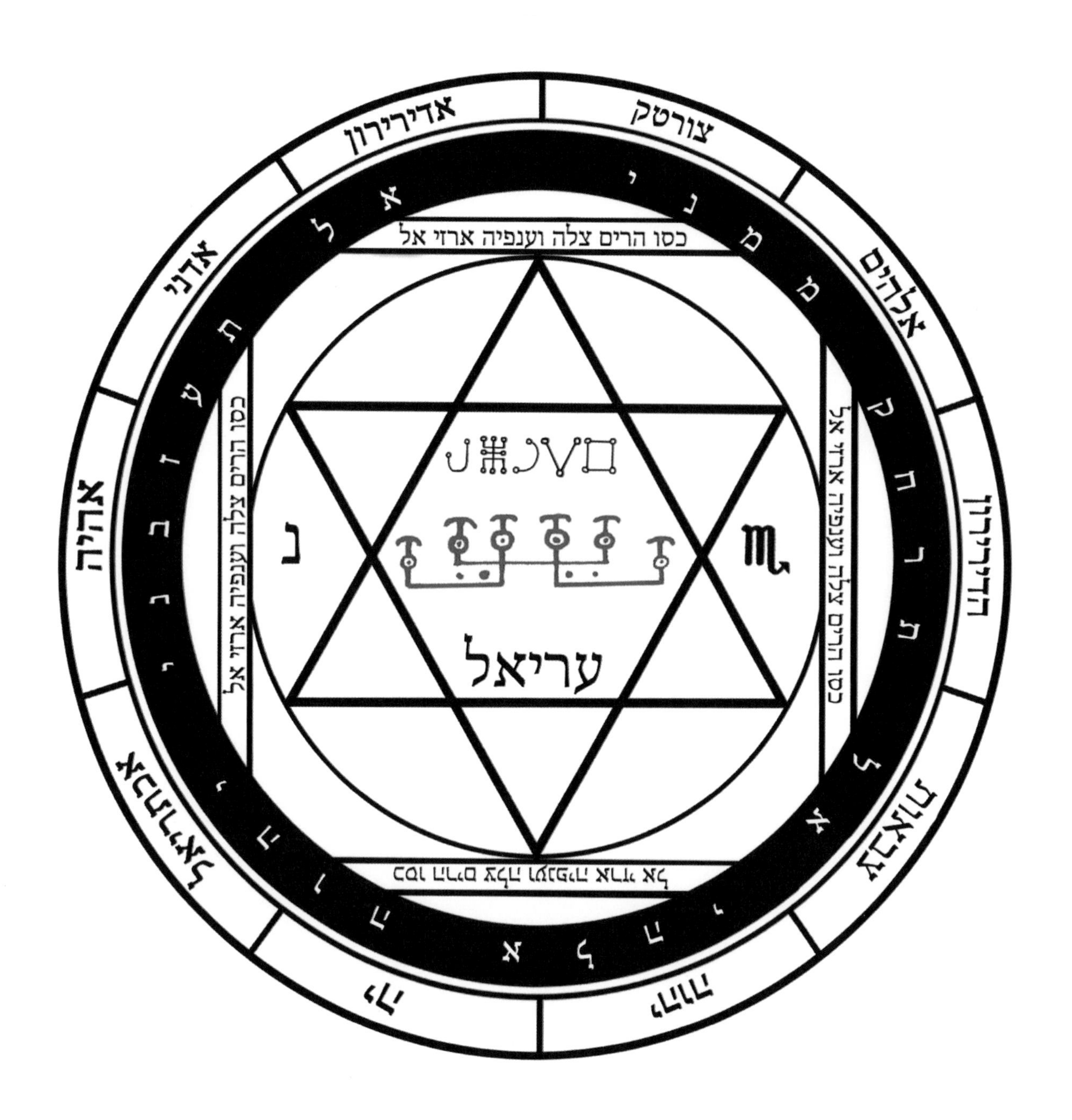

Ariel

AH-REE-ELL

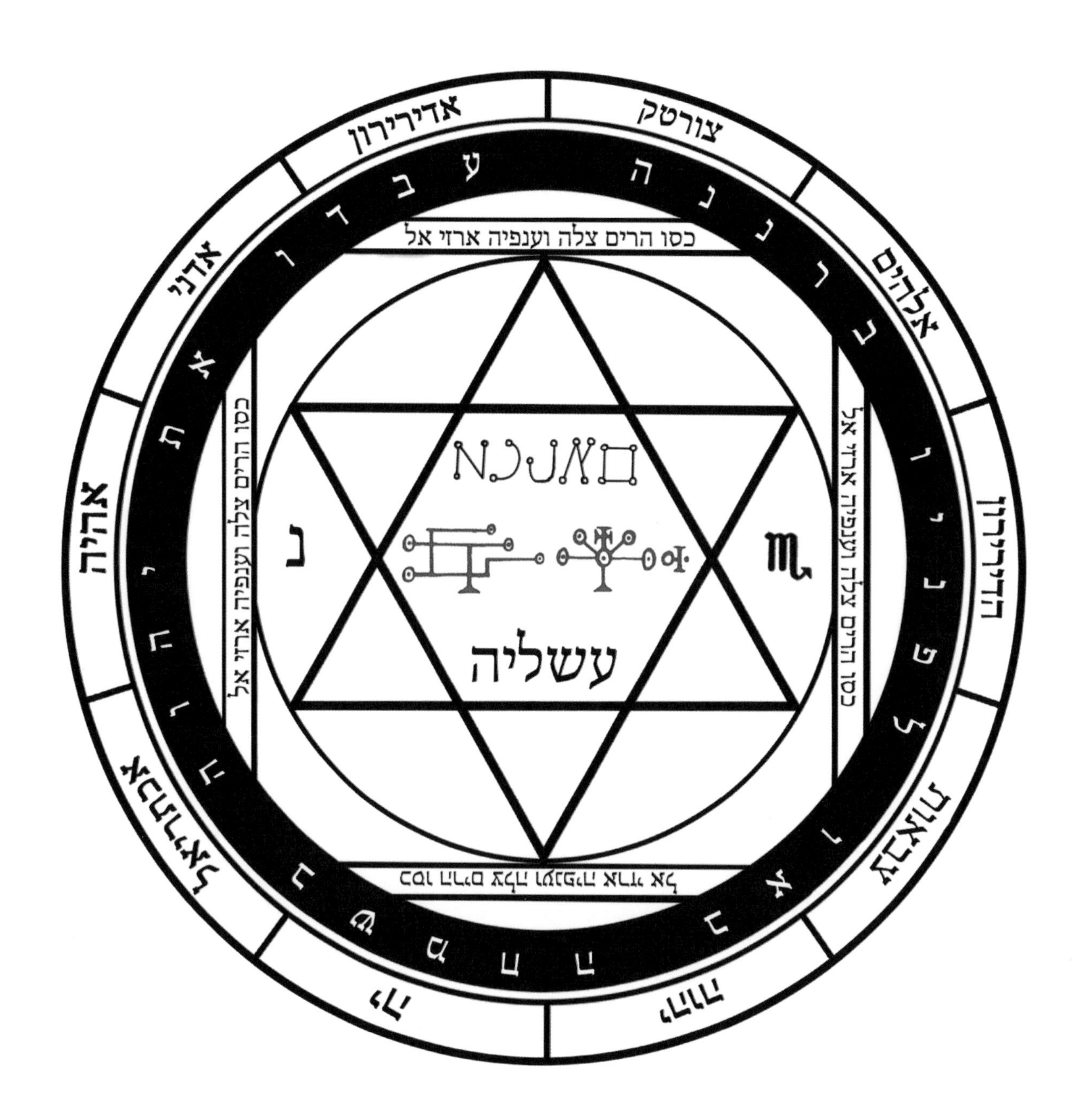

Eshaliah

ESH-AH-LEE-AH

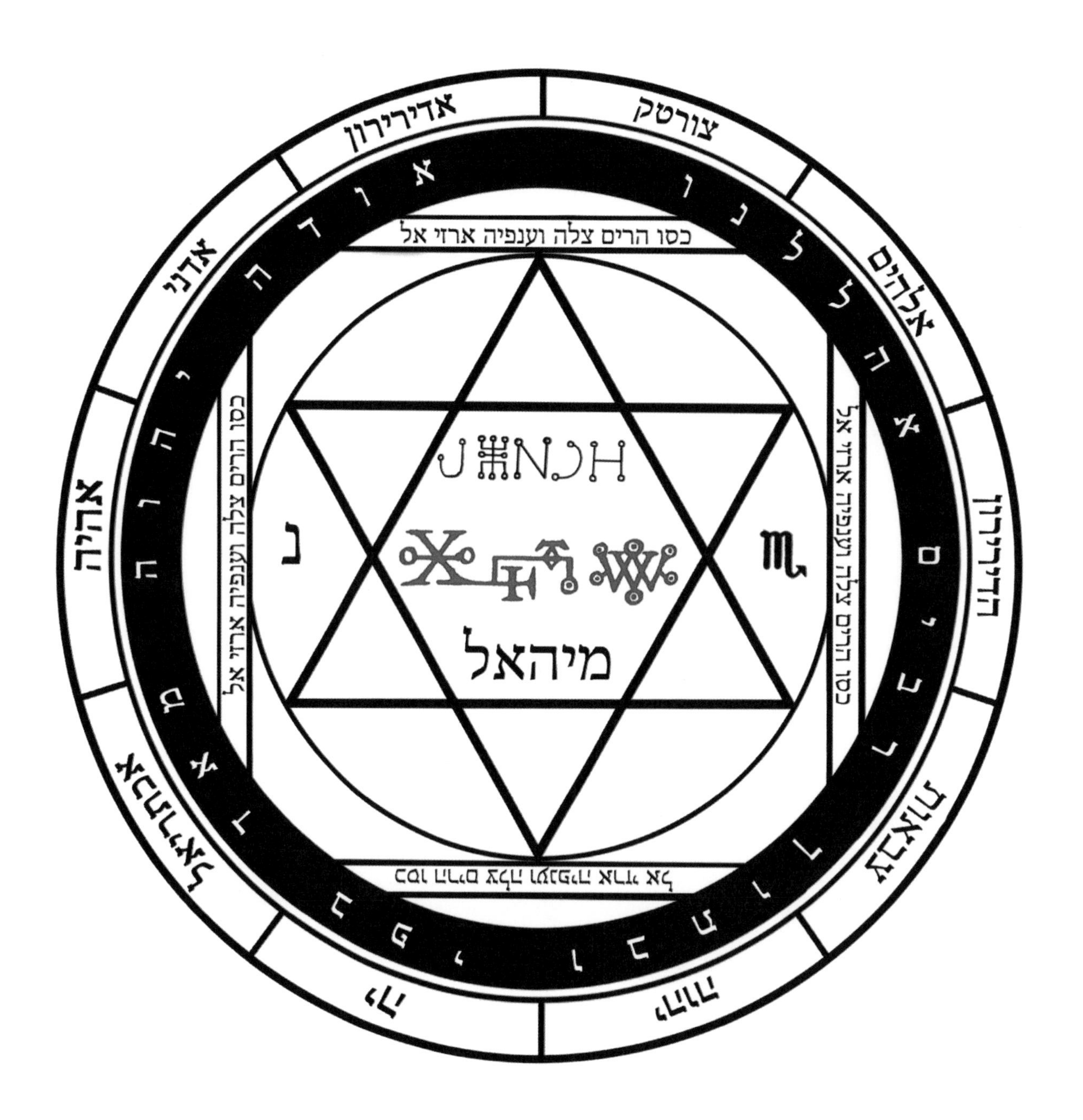

Mihel

ME-HUH-ELL

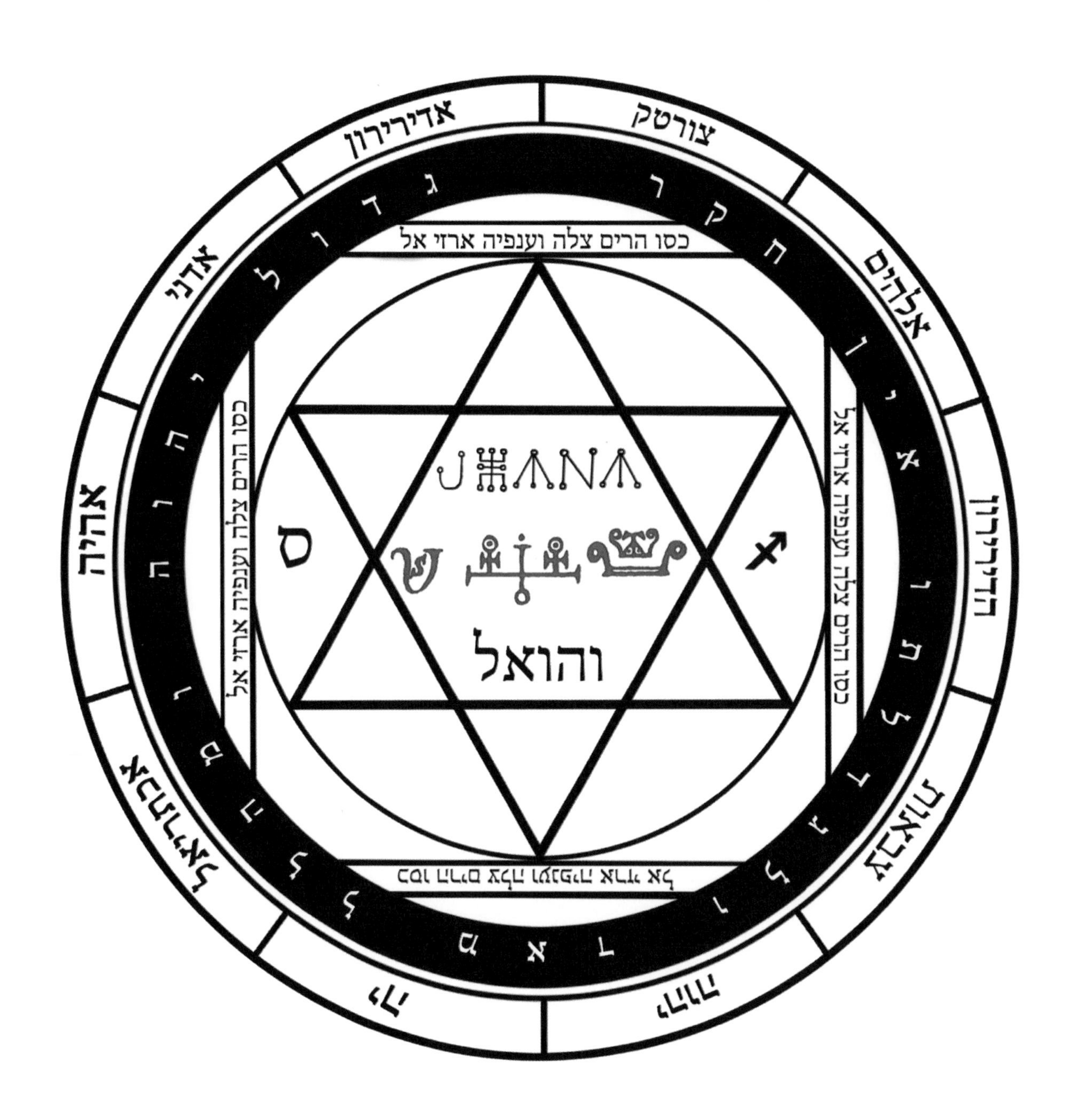

Vehuel

VEH-WHO-ELL

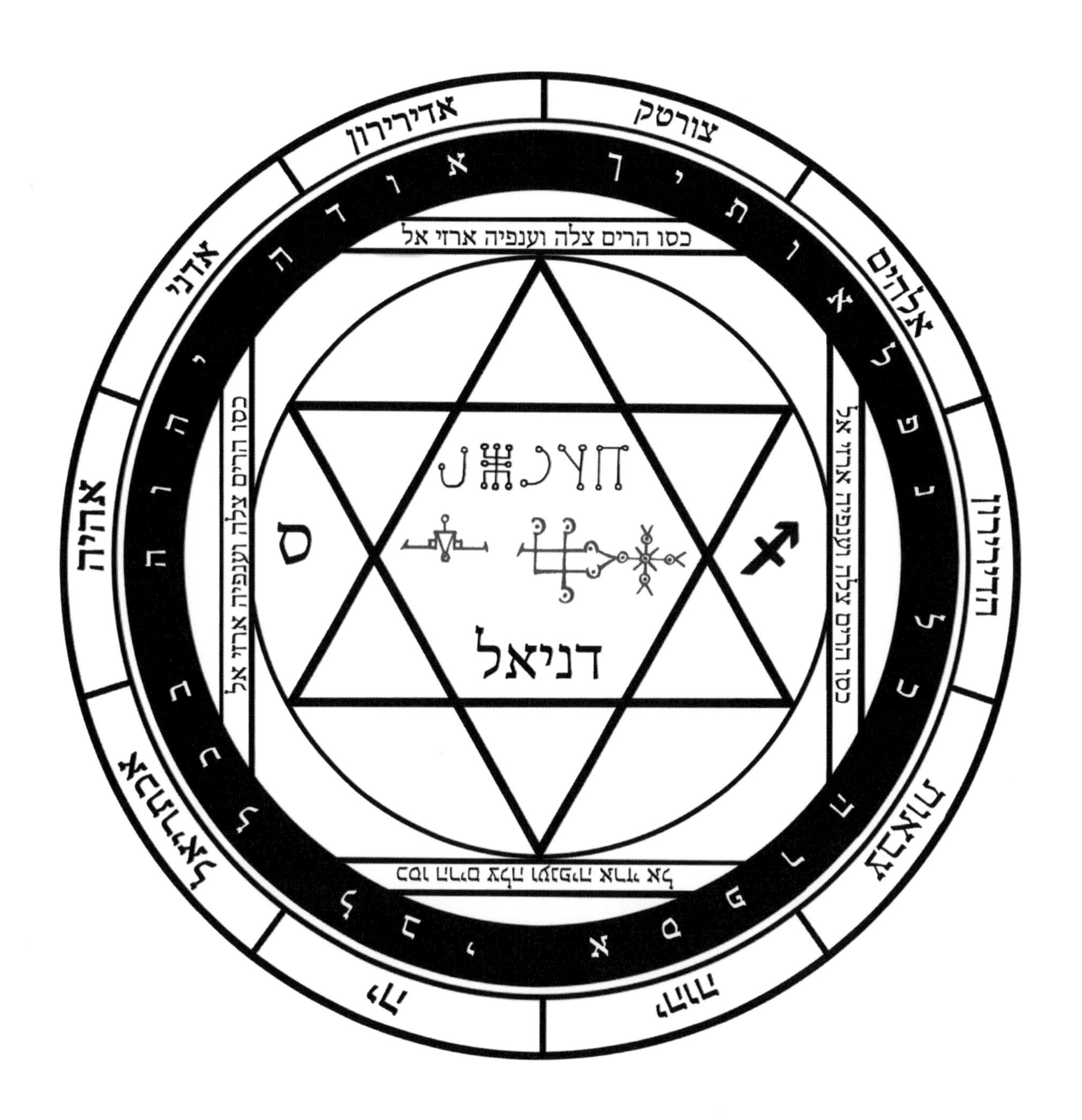

Daniel

DAH-NEE-ELL

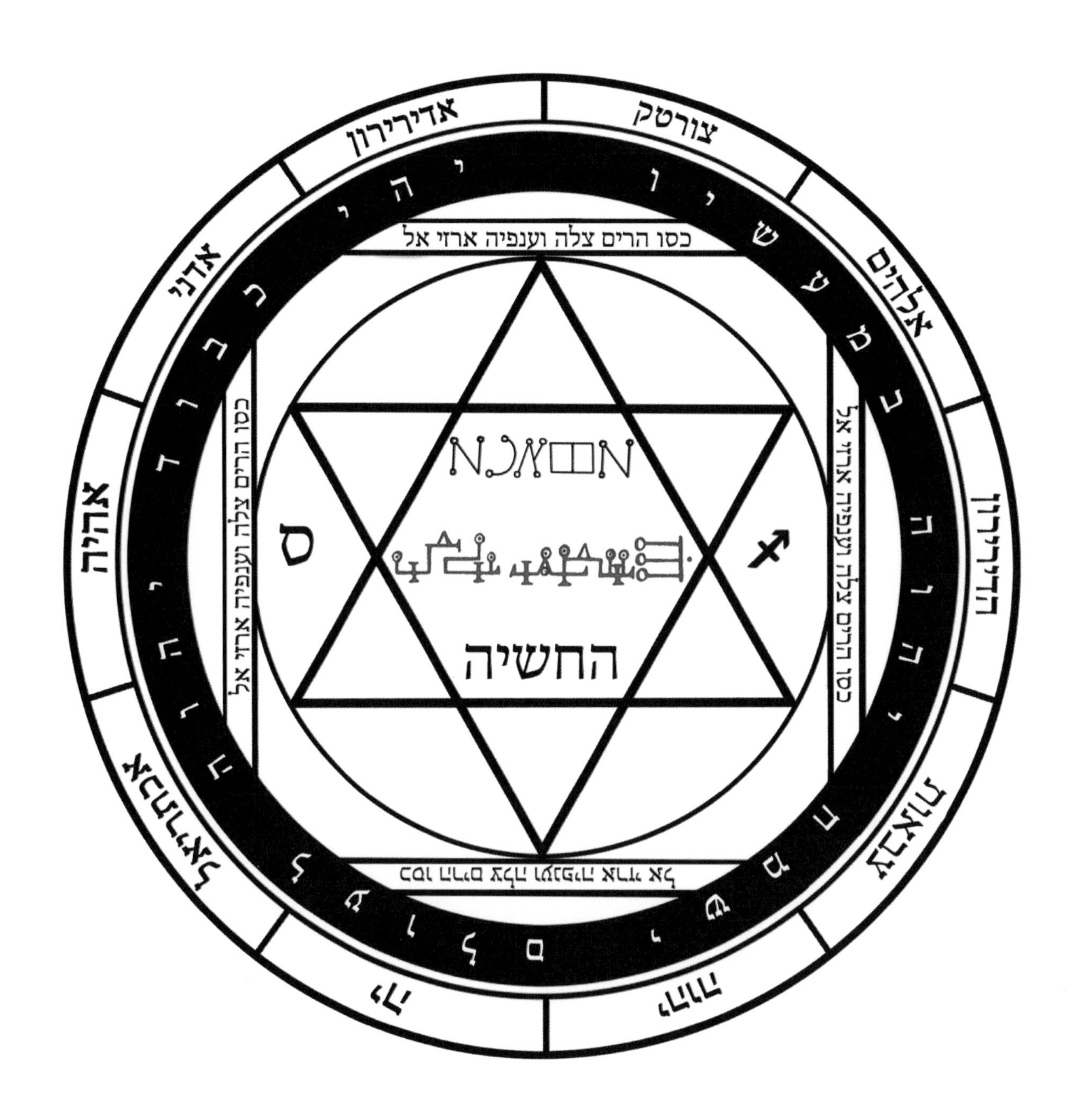

Hachashiah

HAH-CHAH-SHE-YAH

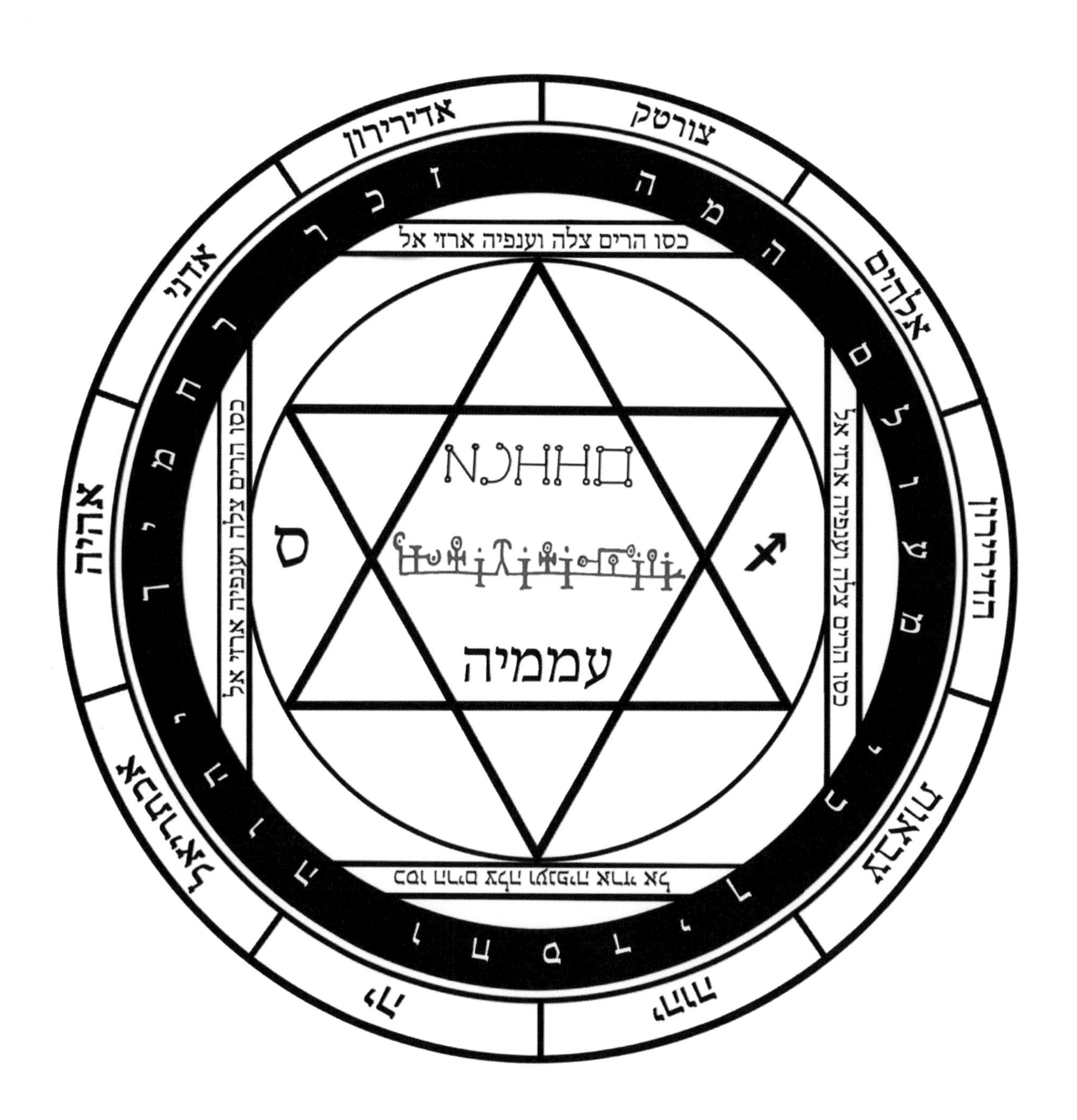

Omemiah

AWE-MEM-EE-AH

Nenael

NEN-AH-ELL

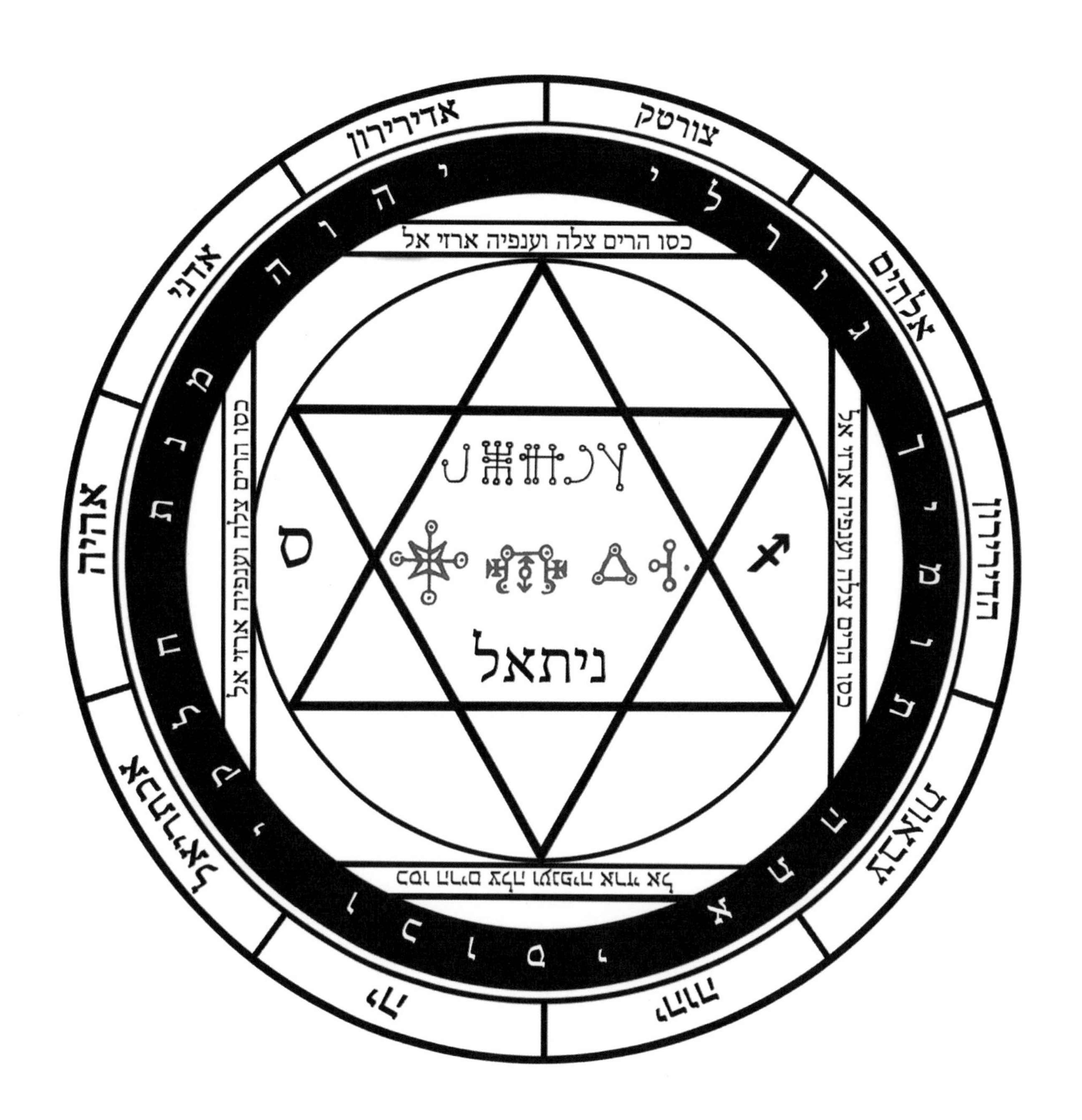

Nitel

NEAT-UH-ELL

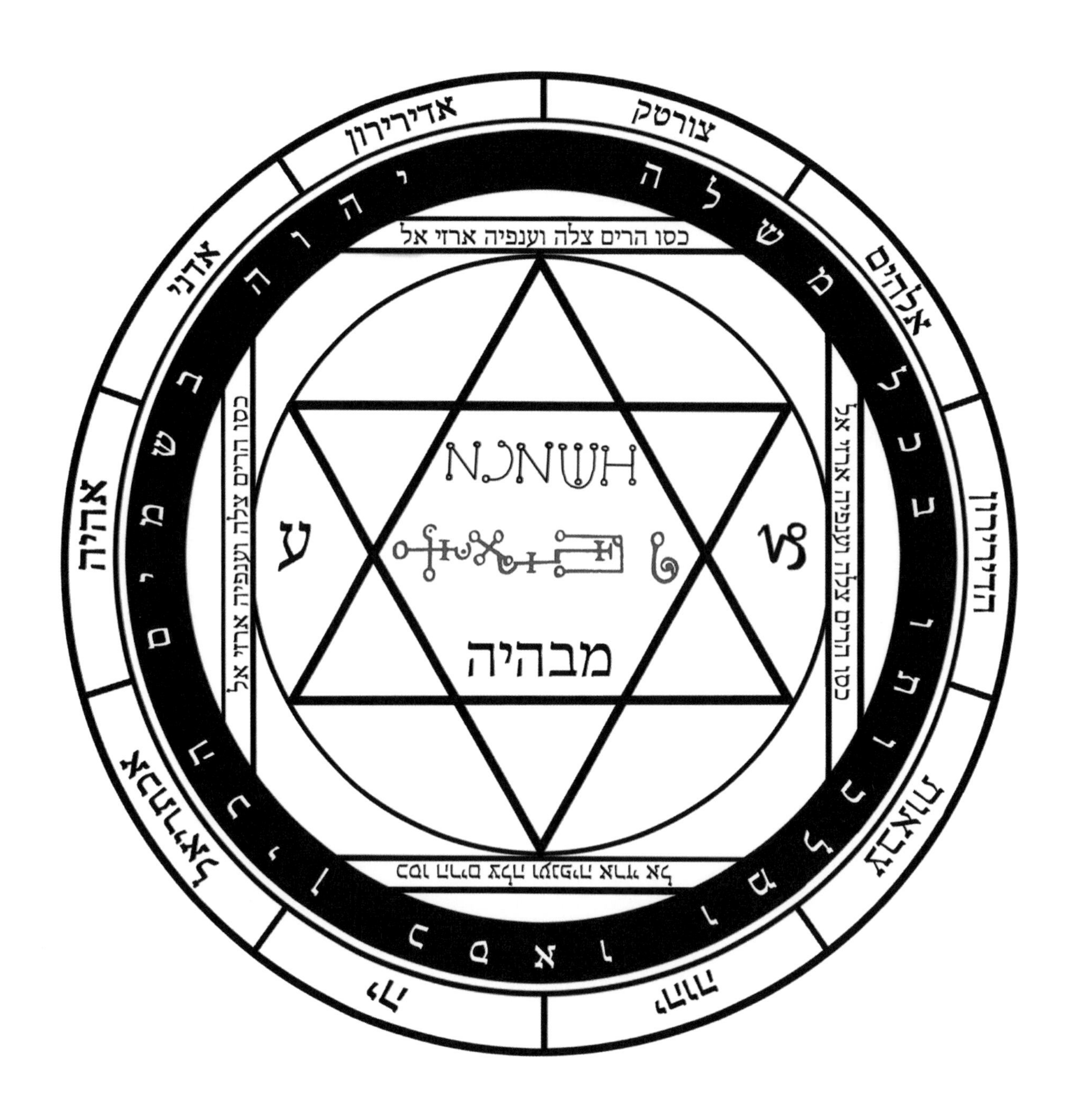

Mivahiah

ME-VAH-HEE-AH

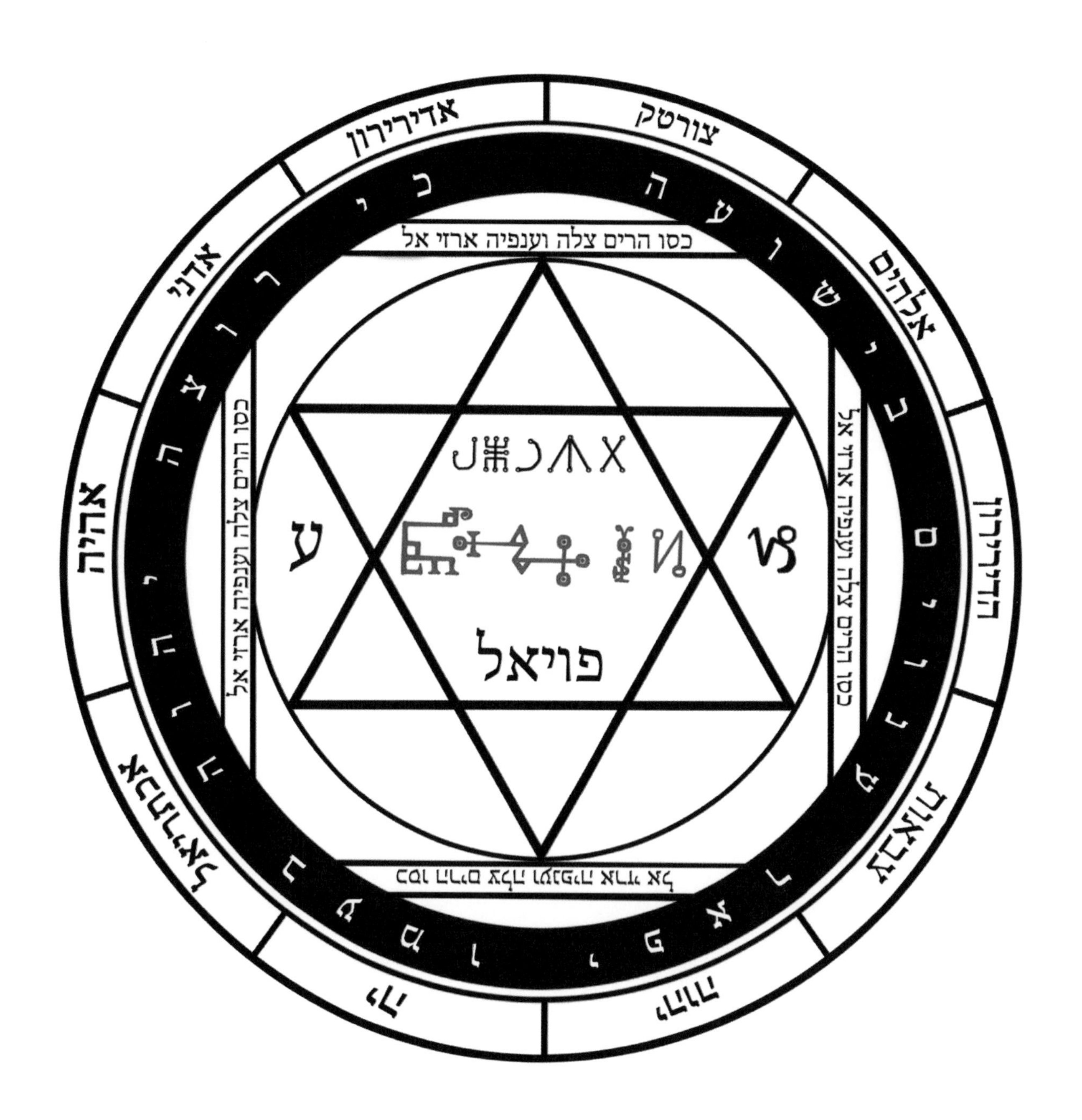

Poiel

PAW-EE-ELL

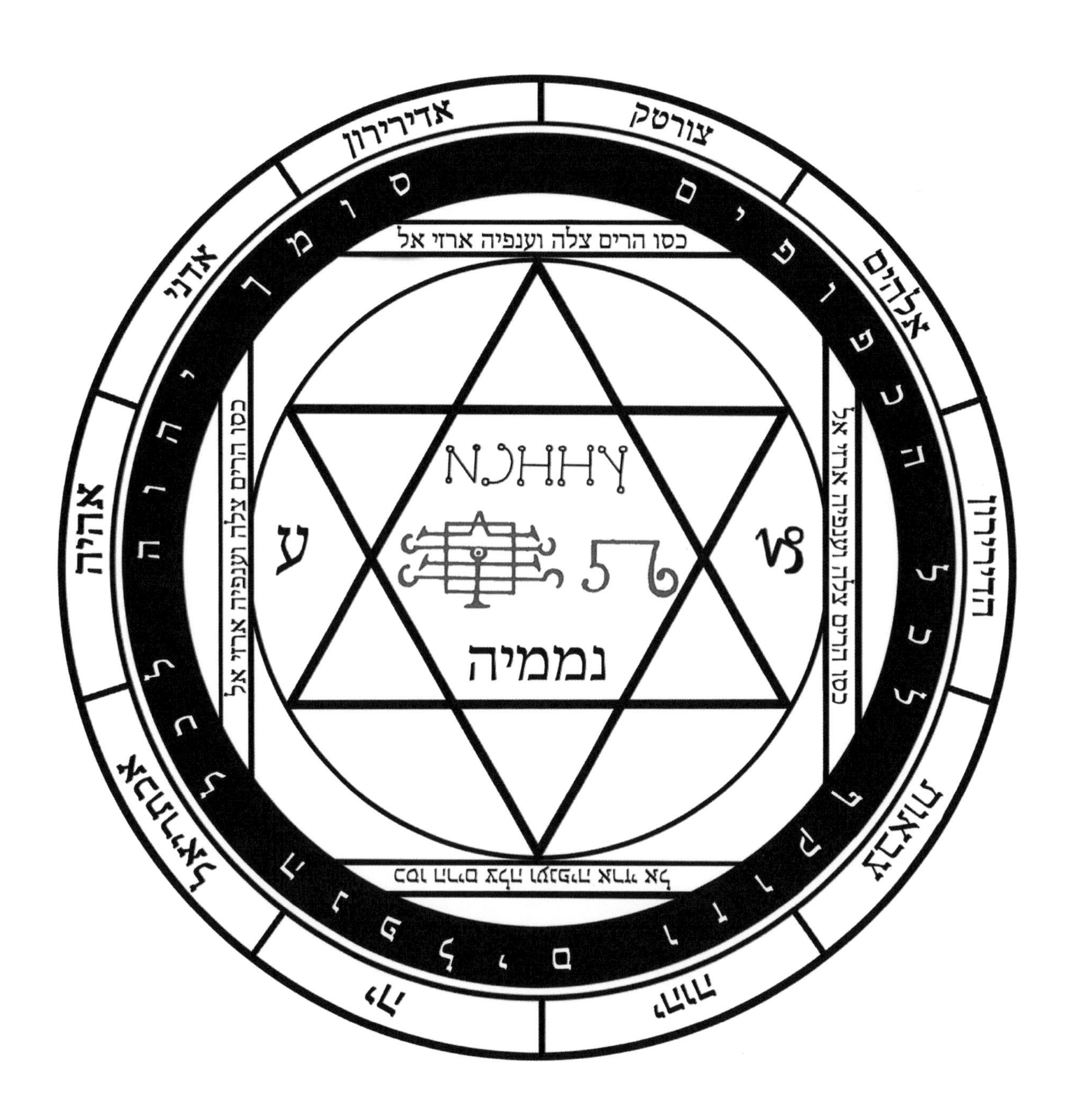

Nememiah

NEM-EM-EE-AH

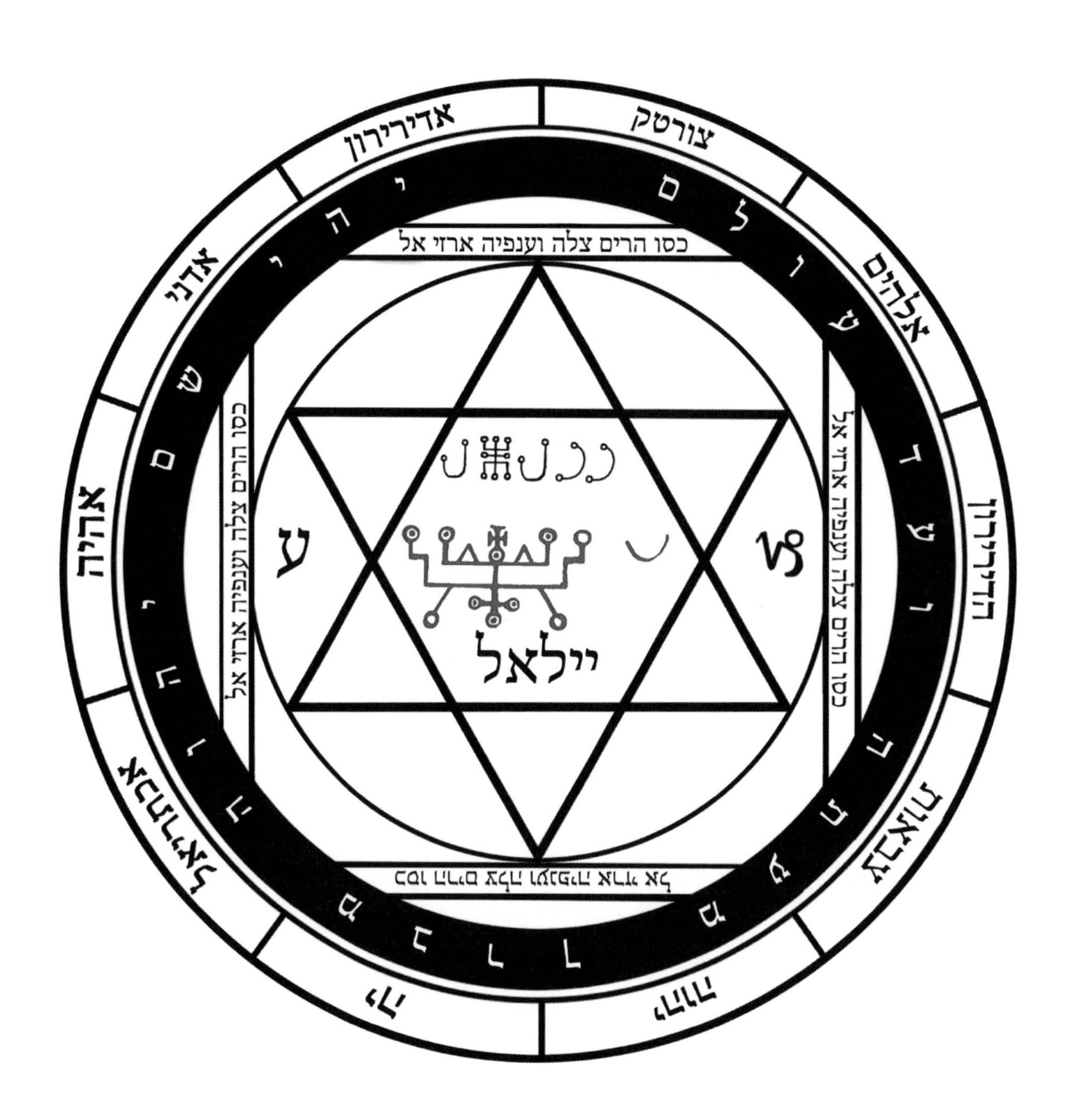

Yeyilel

YEH-YEE-LUH-ELL

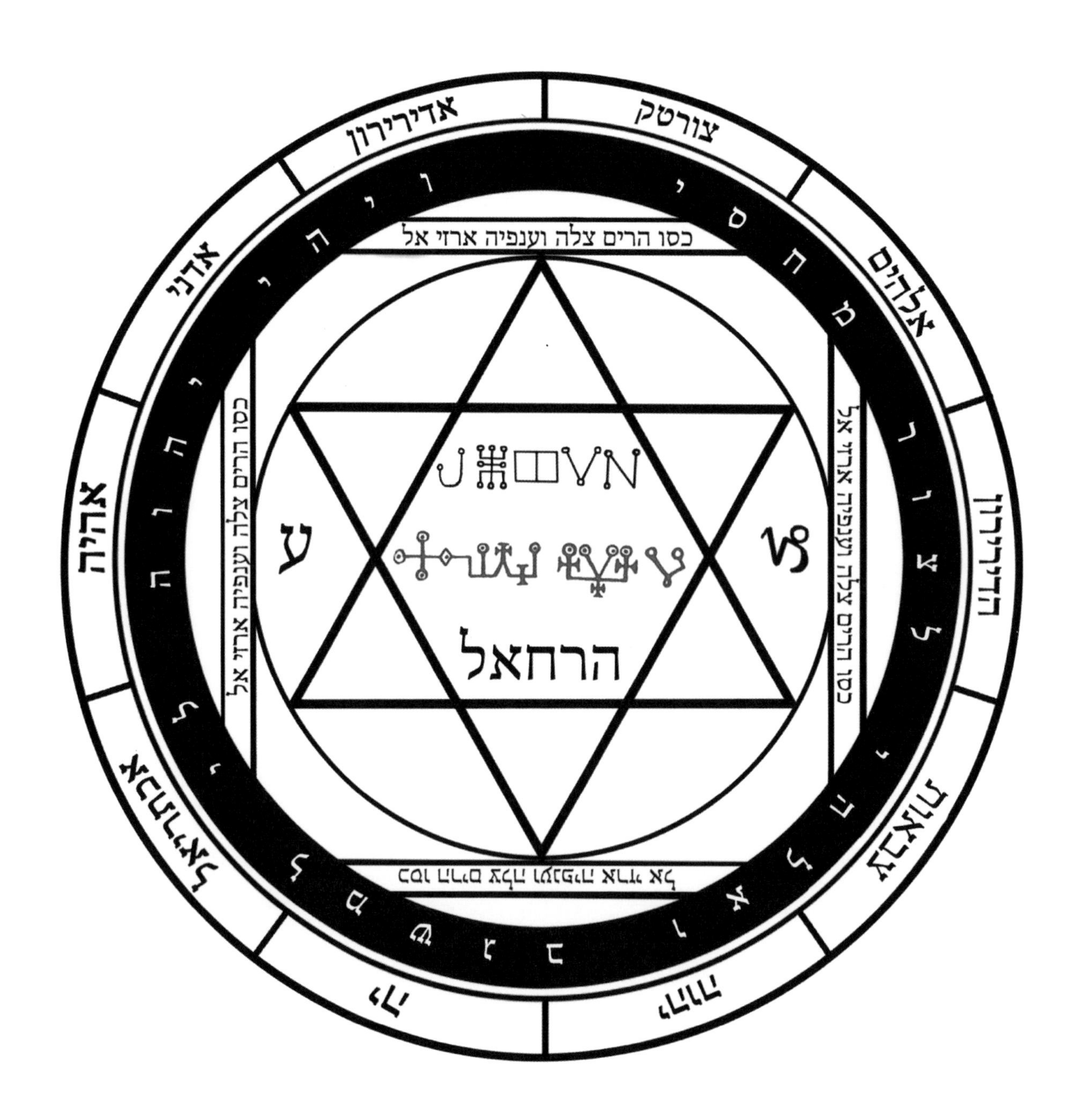

Harachel

HAH-RAH-CHELL

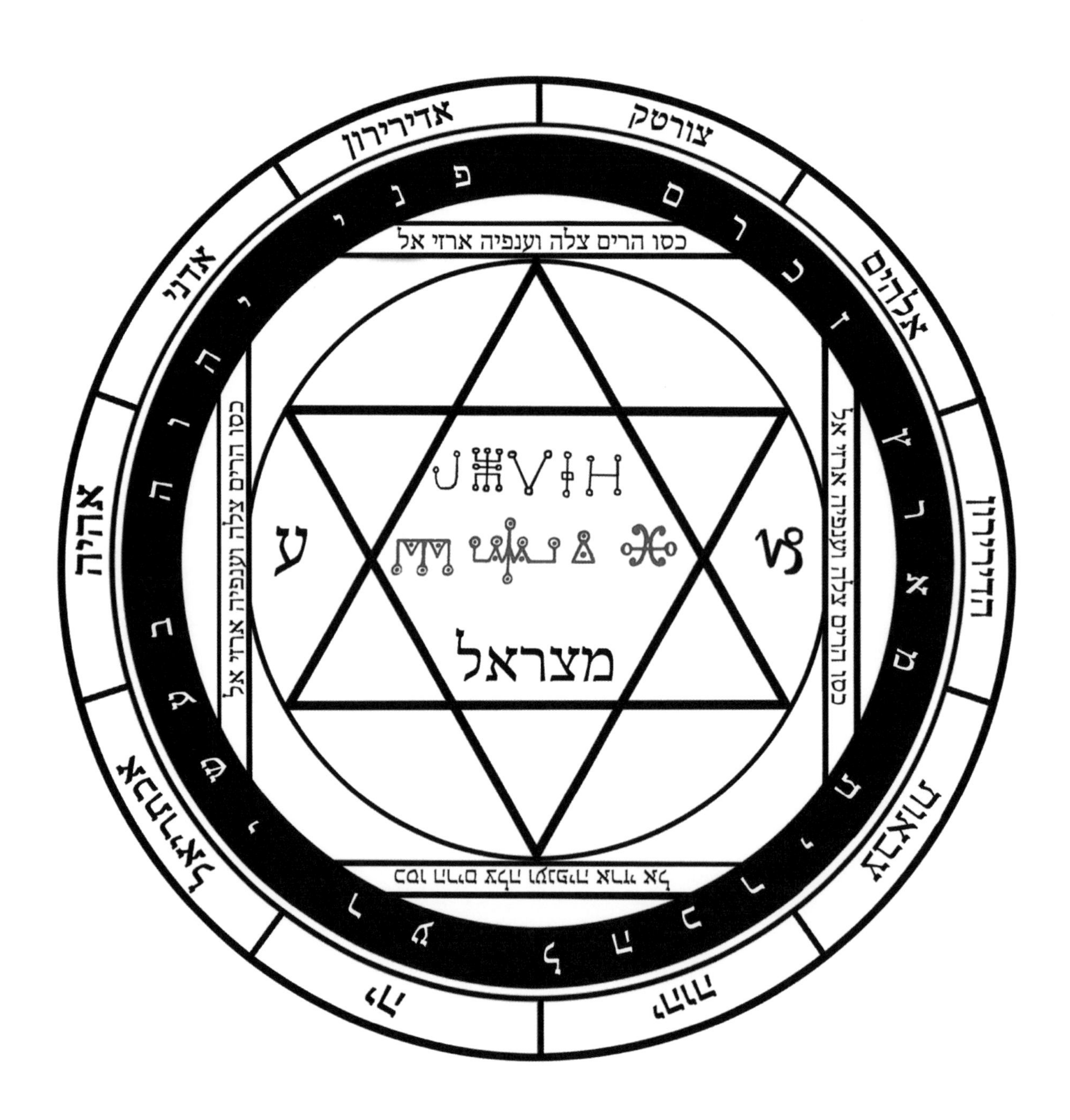

Metzerel

MET-ZEH-RELL

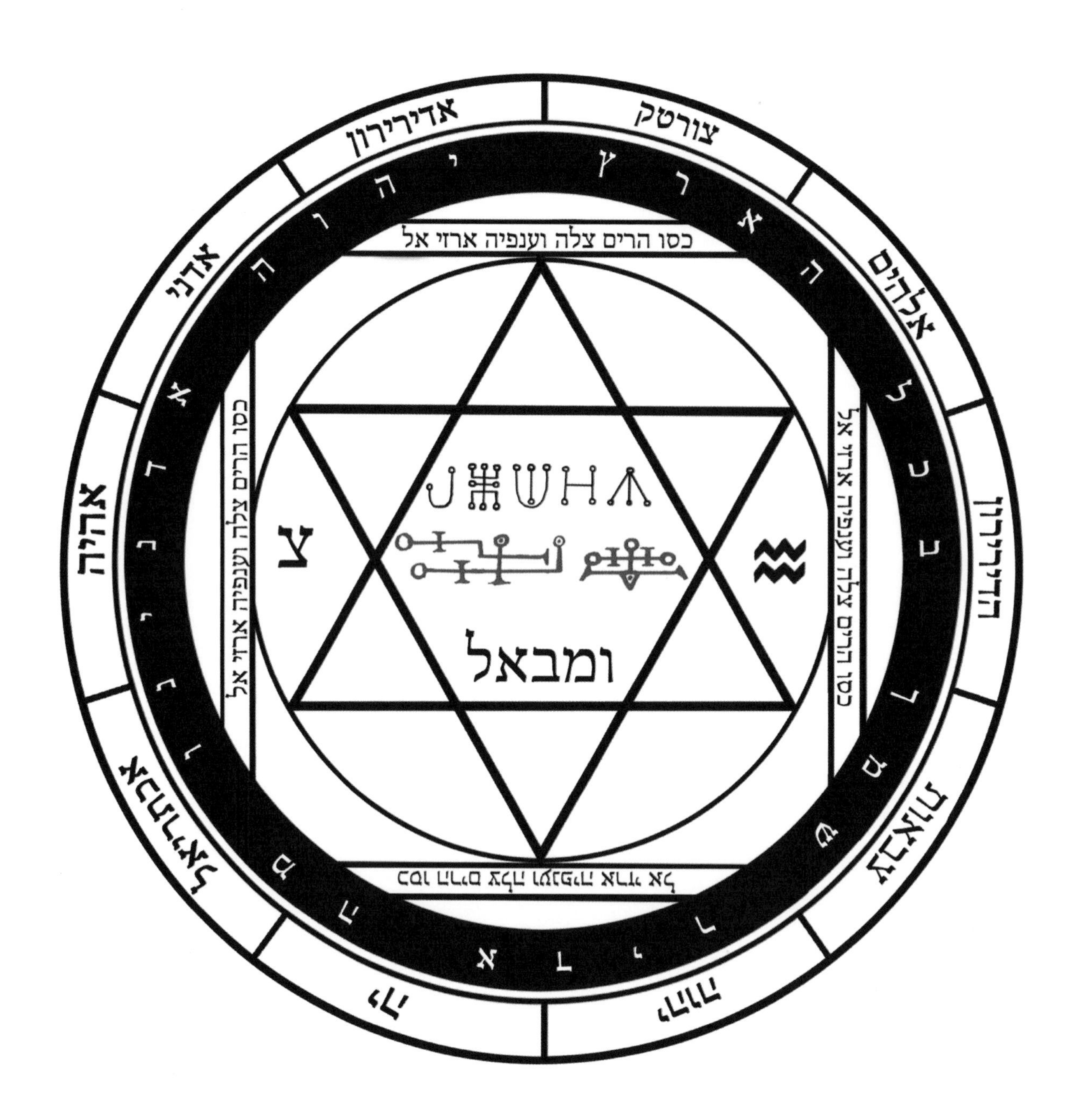

Umabel

OOM-AB-ELL

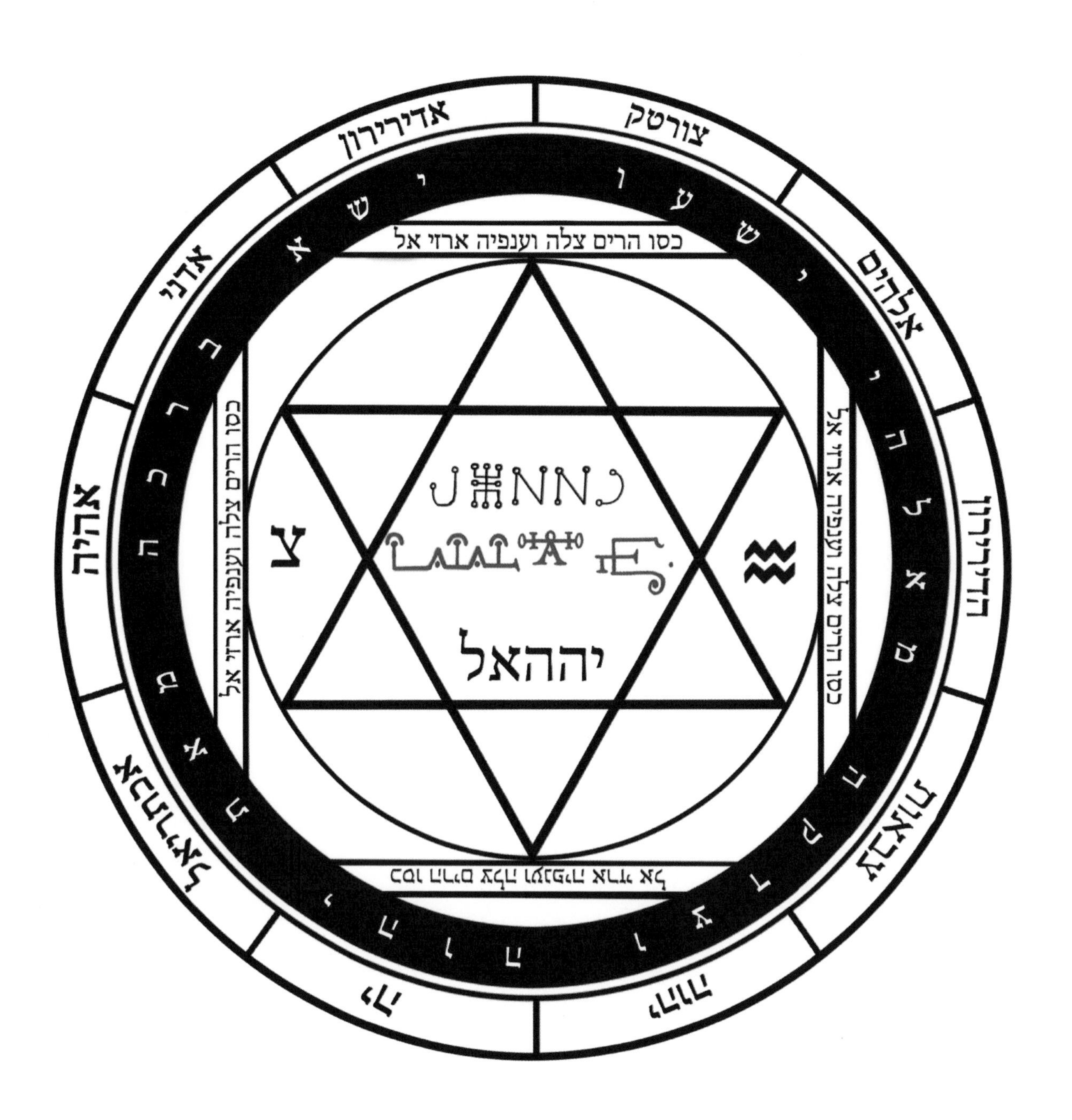

Yahahel

YAH-AH-ELL

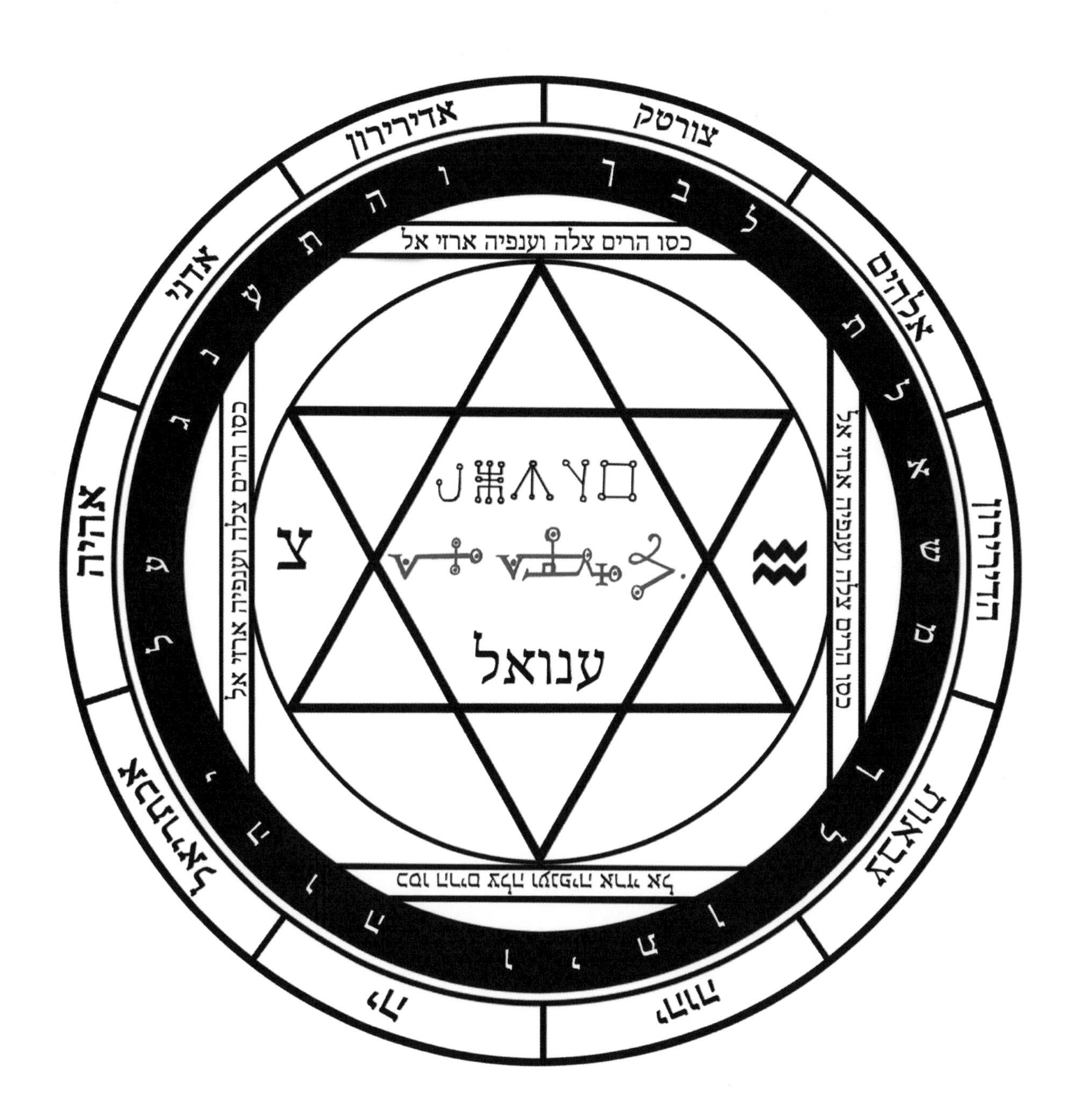

Anuel

AH-NOO-ELL

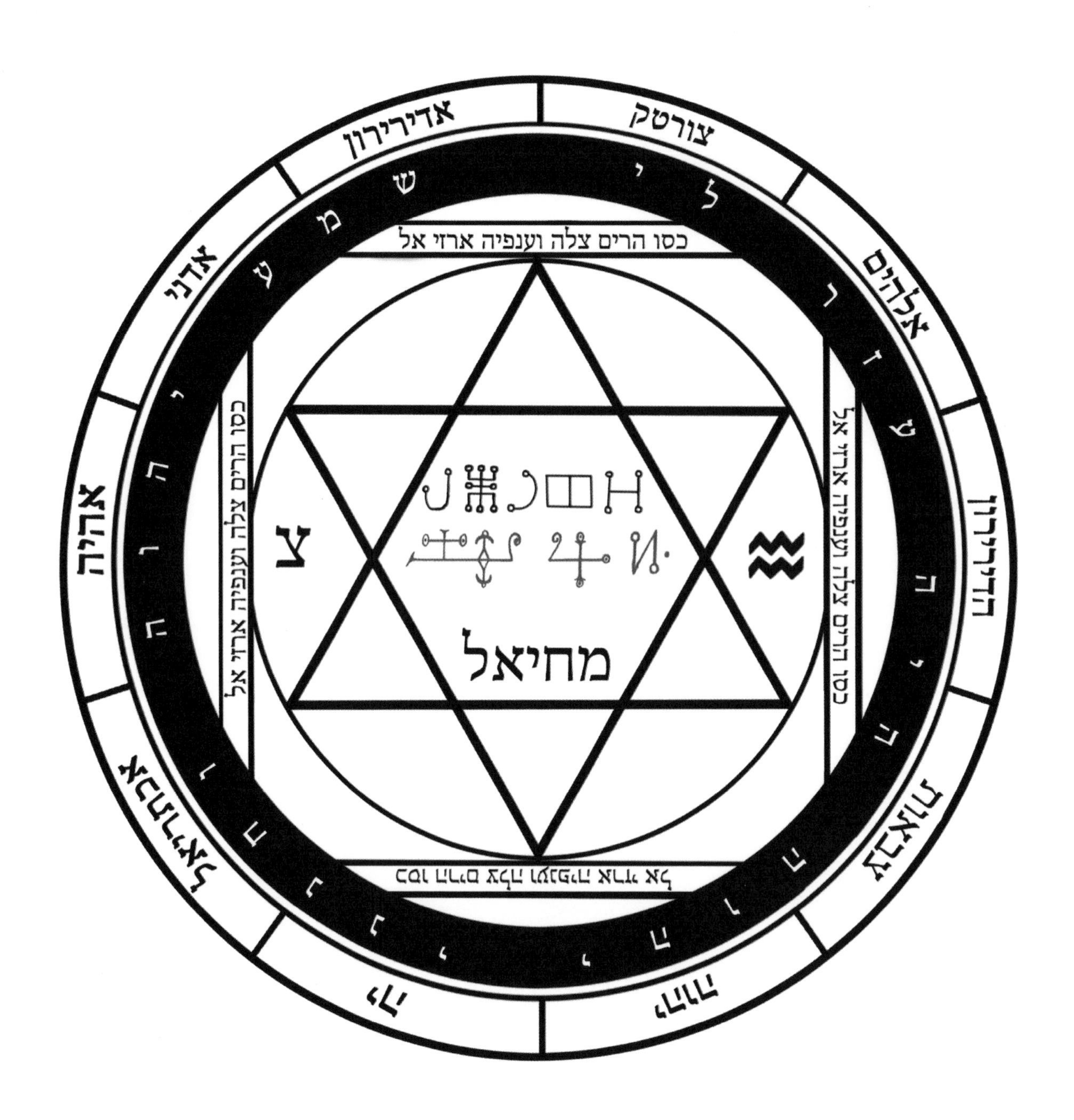

Machiel

MAH-CHEE-ELL

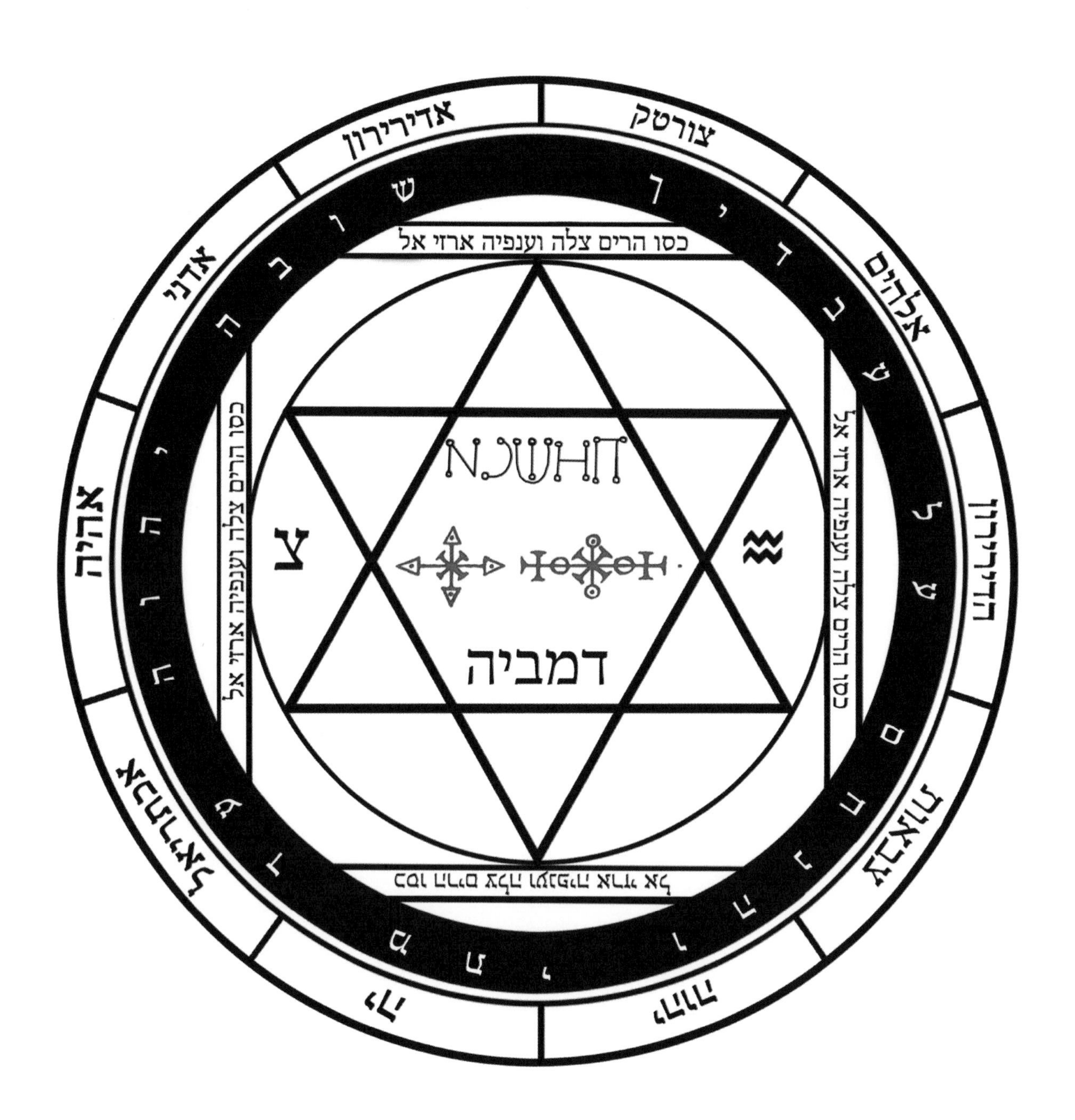

Damebiah

DAM-EH-BEE-AH

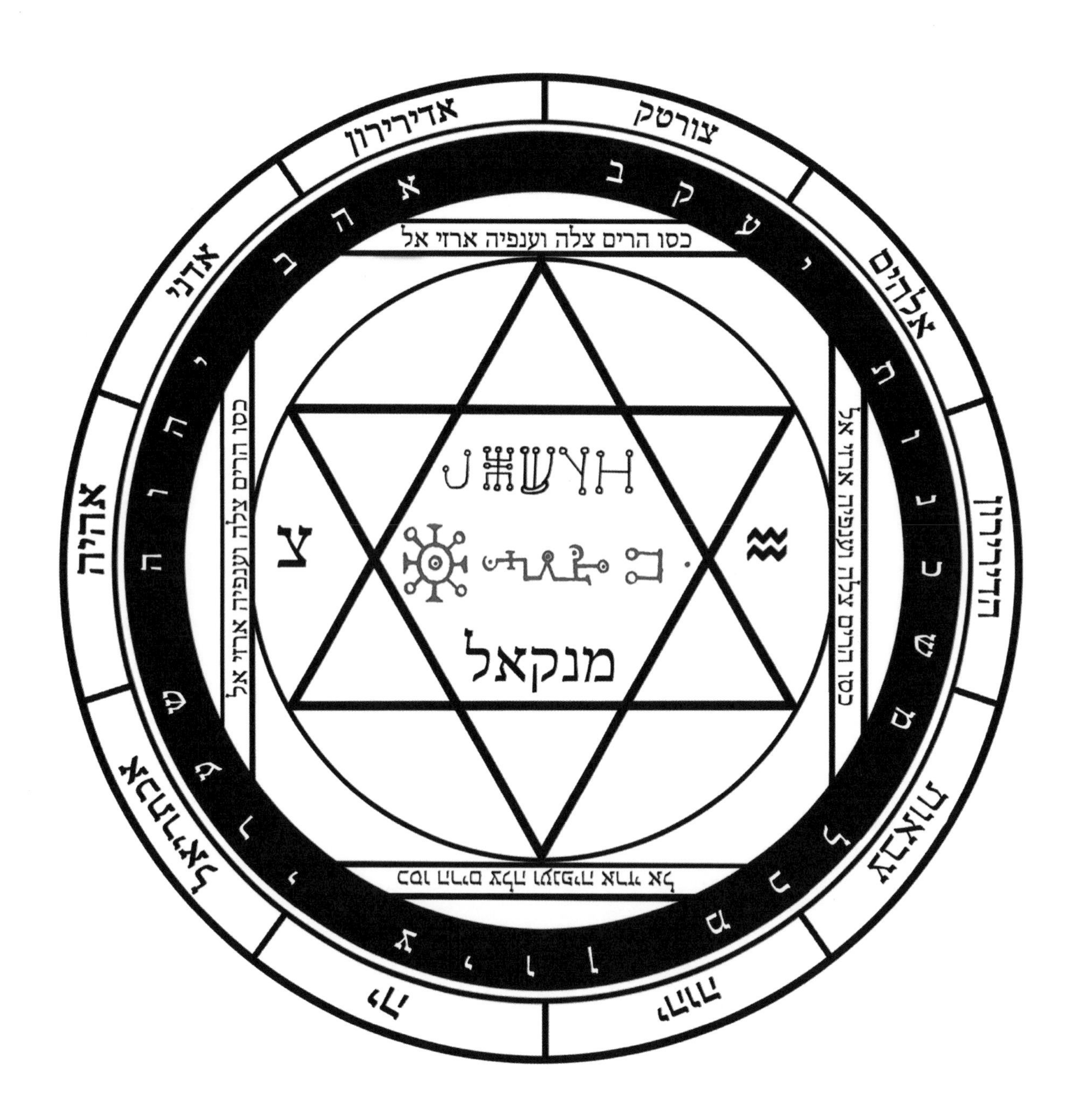

Menakel

MEN-AH-KELL

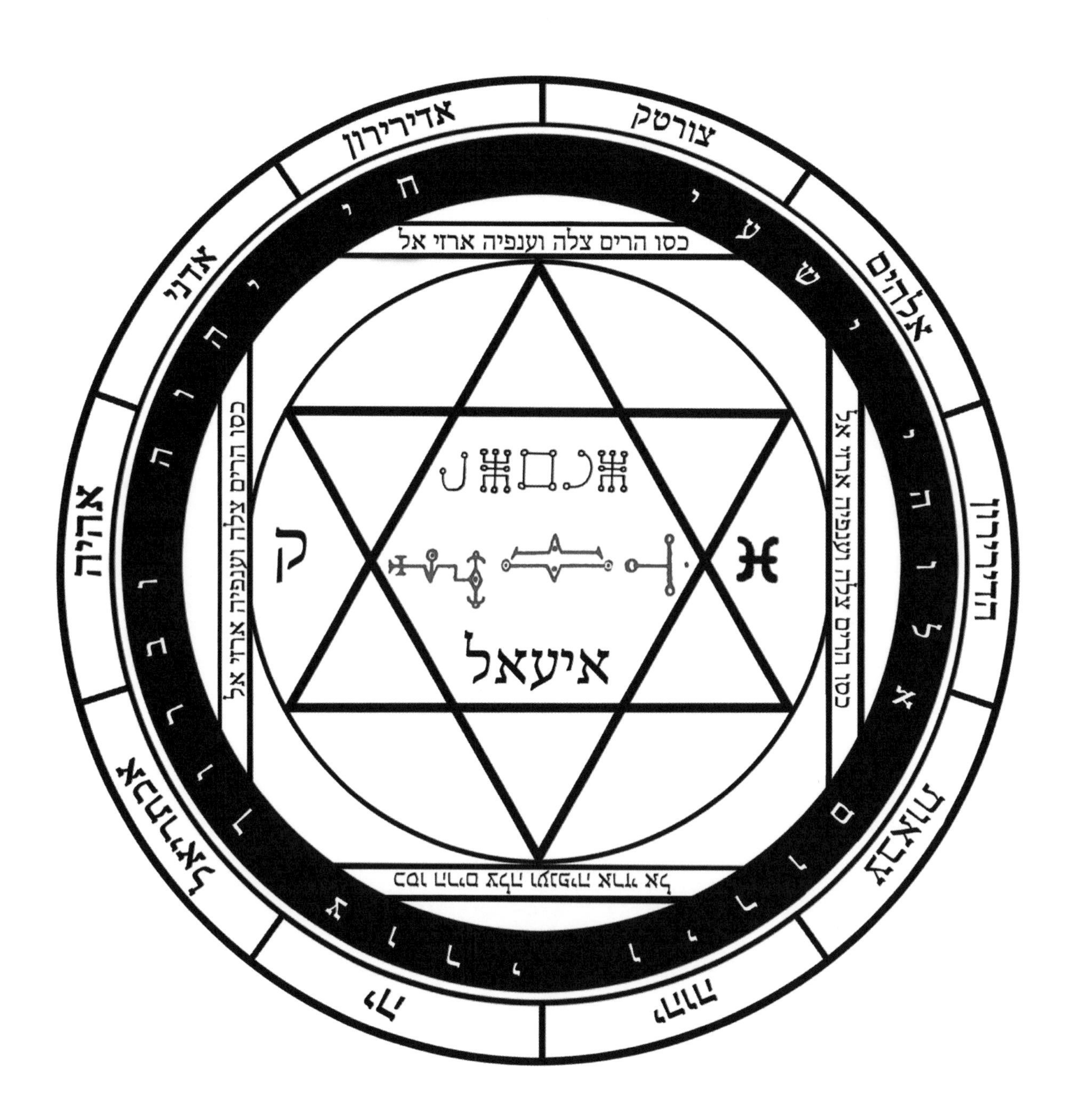

Iyahel

EE-AH-ELL

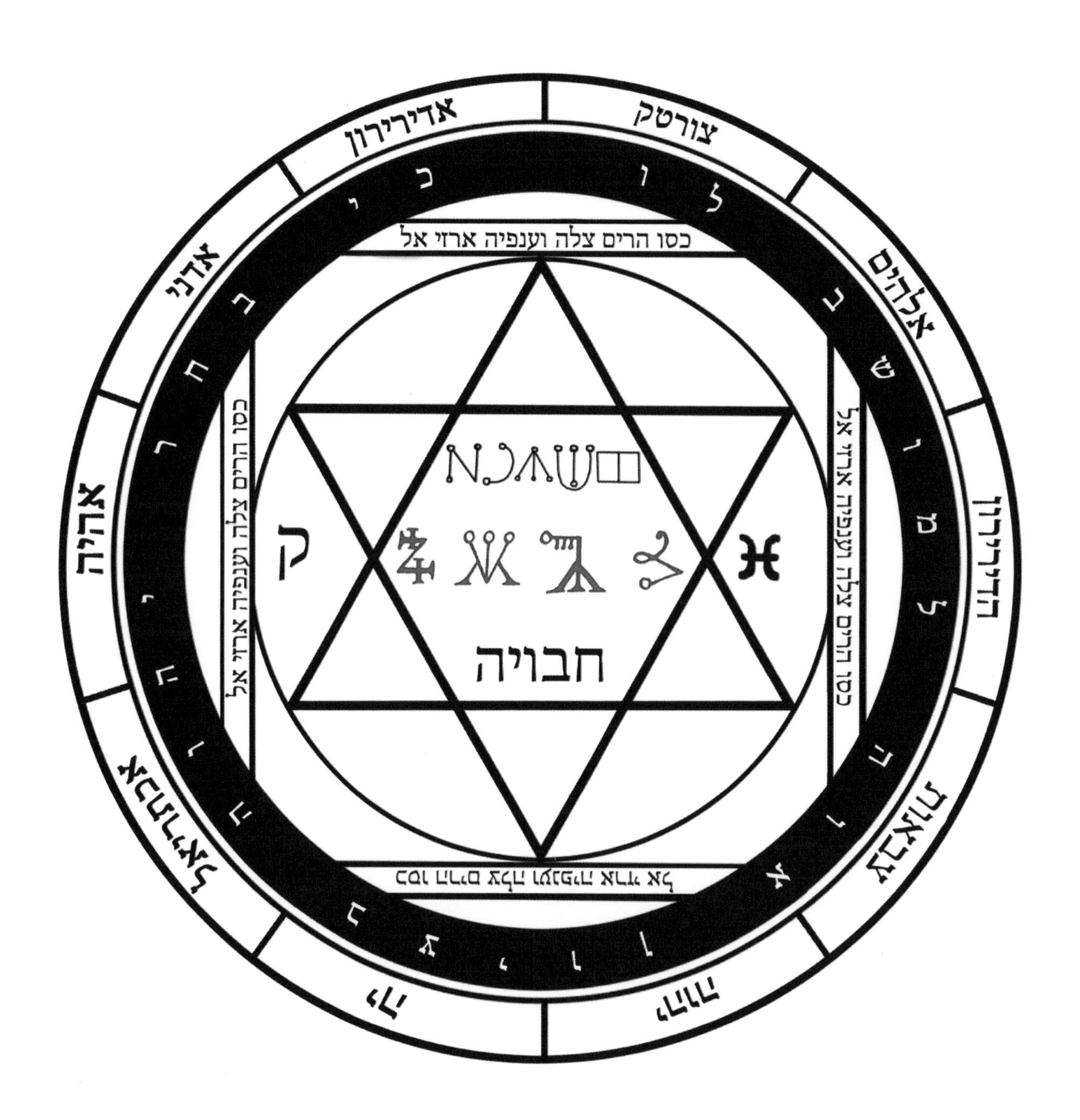

Chavuiah

CHAH-VOO-EE-AH

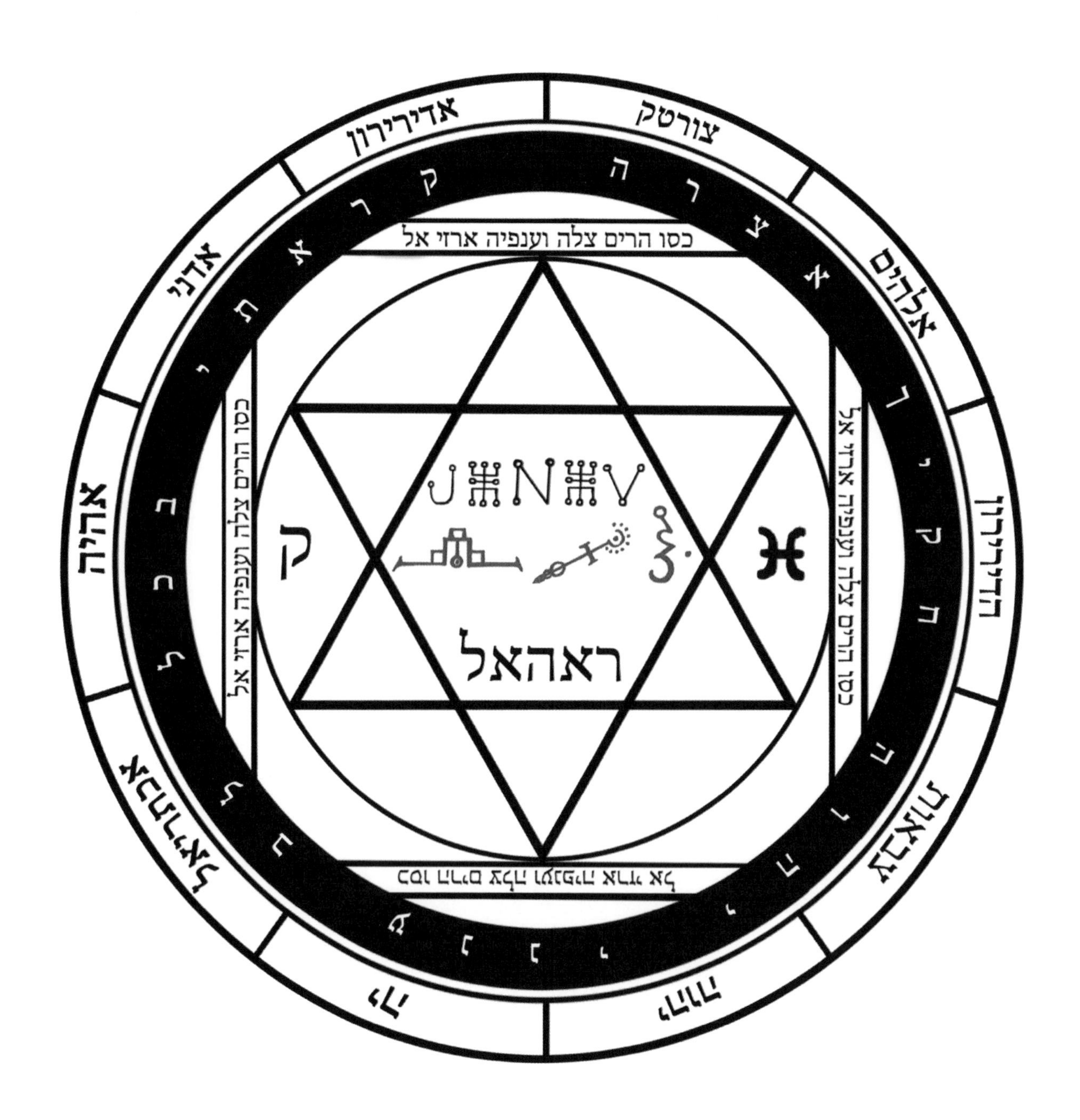

Raahel

RAH-AH-ELL

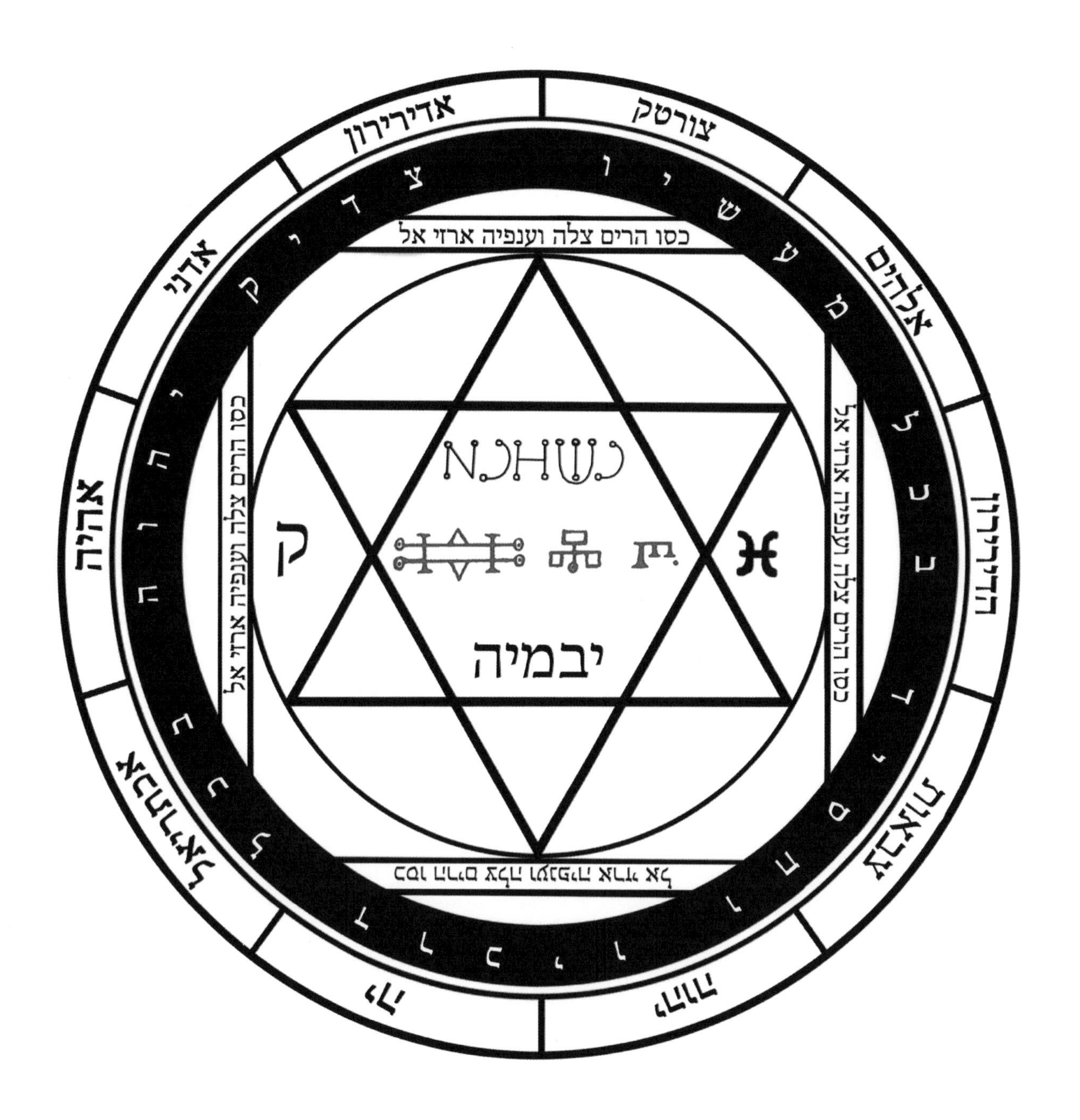

Yabamiah

YAH-BAH-ME-AH

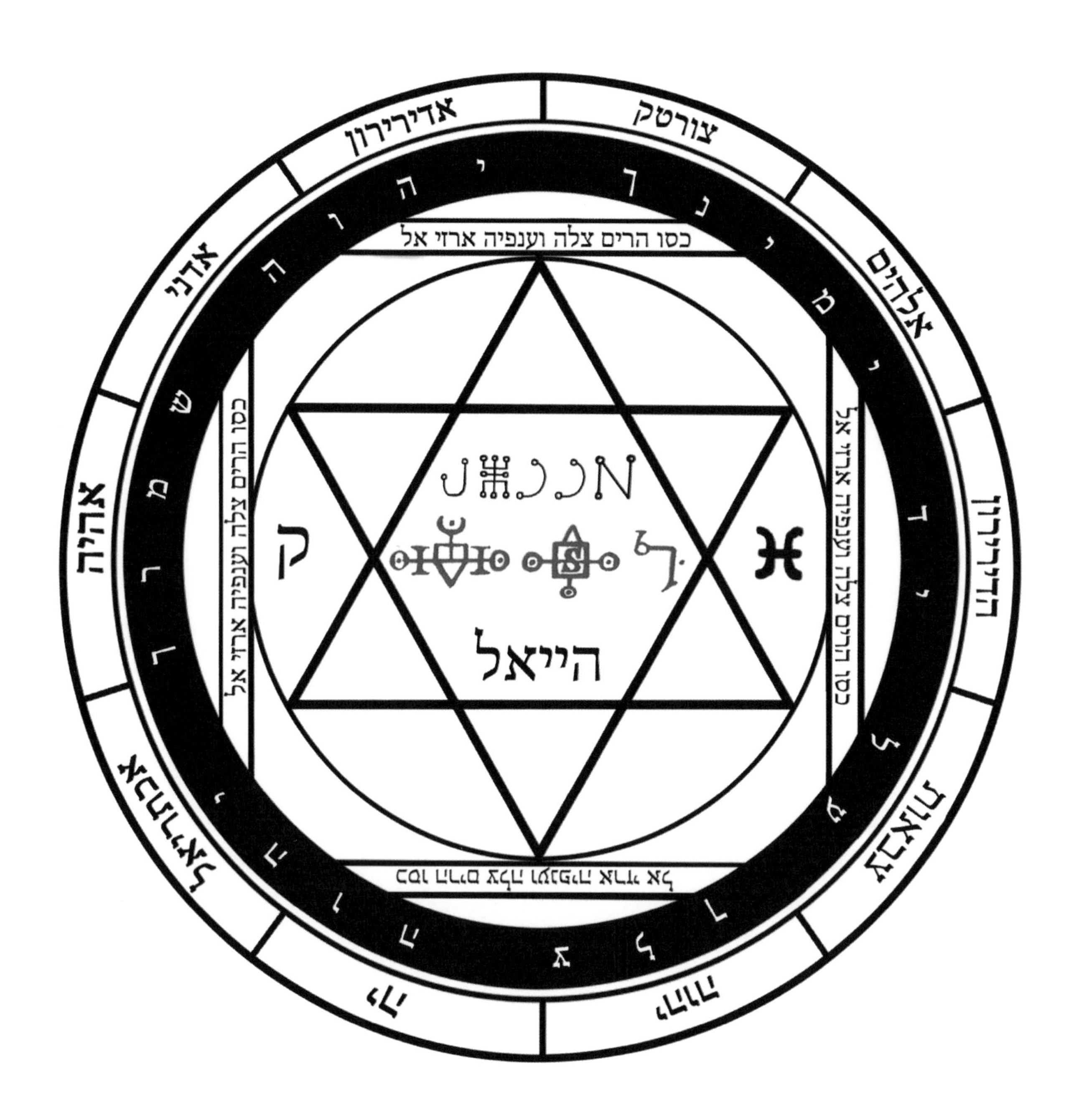

Hayiel

HAH-YEE-ELL

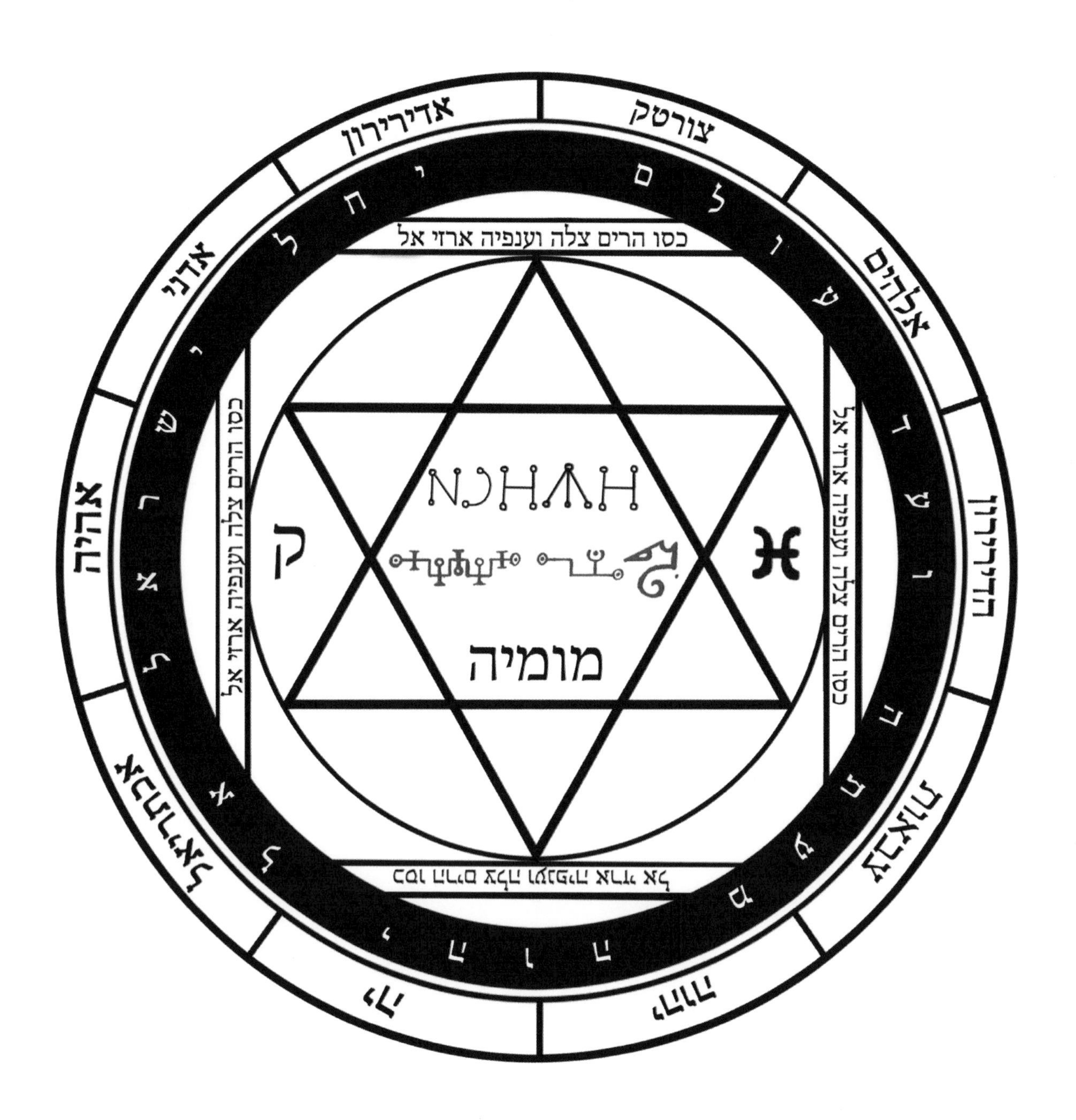

Mumiah

MOOM-EE-AH

Images from *Magickal Riches*

The sigil for The Master Money Ritual appears in its original form, and in color. Some people find that using the color version helps with the visual aspect of the associated ritual. Others like to cut out the sigil and keep in to close while they work on financial projects.

Individual, physical copies of the other sigils can make it easier to work the magick. The square sigils, which call on the genius spirits, can all be arranged in front of you before you begin the ritual, for example, which is easier than flipping from page to page as you work.

גבריאל סודיאל רומיאל חסדיאל שמריאל

מיכאל רפאל
צדקיאל פניאל
רחמיאל נוריאל
רזיאל יופיאל
יהו יהו יהו יהו יהו יהו
שמשיאל יחואל

אוריאל זכריאל יהואל מלטיאל רזיאל

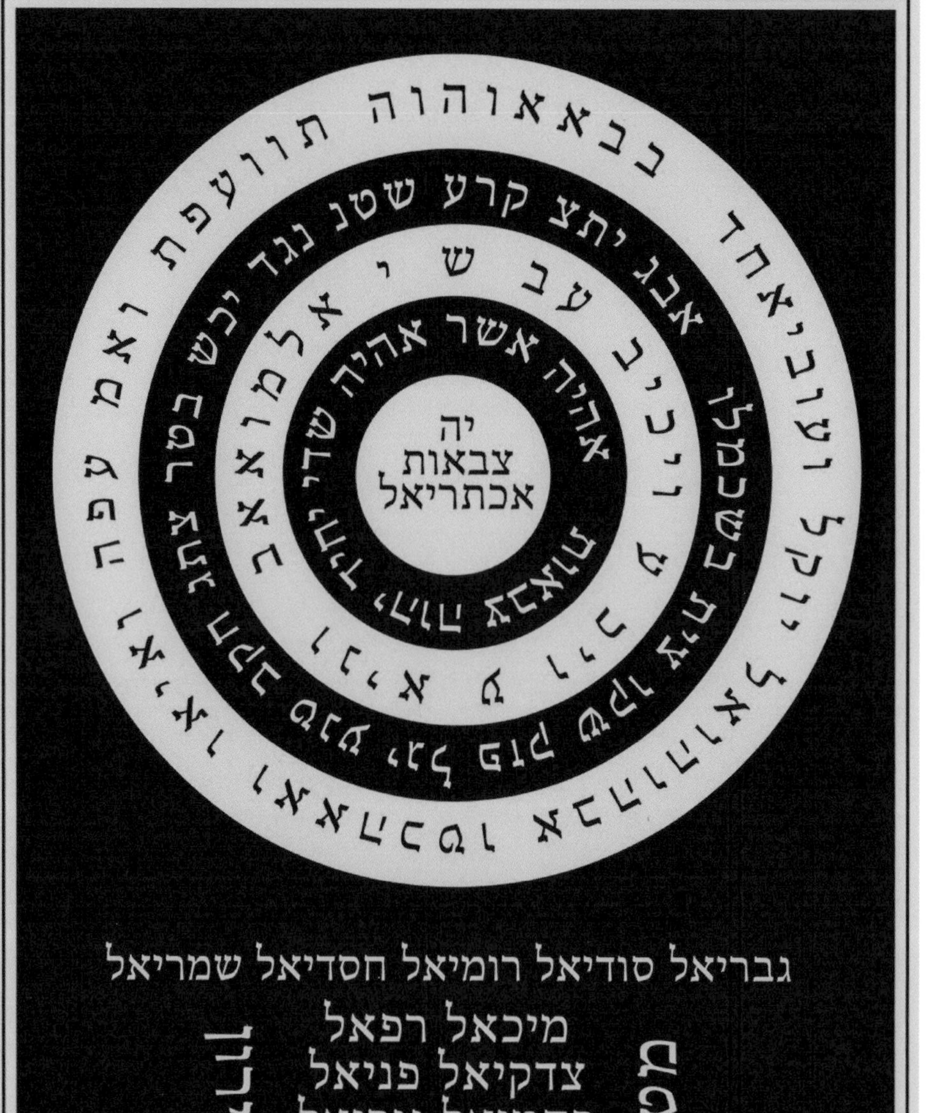

גבריאל סודיאל רומיאל חסדיאל שמריאל

מיכאל רפאל
צדקיאל פניאל
רחמיאל נוריאל
רזיאל יופיאל
יהו יהו יהו יהו יהו יהו
שמשיאל יחואל

אוריאל זכריאל יהואל מלטיאל רזיאל

אהיה אשר אהיה

אדירירון

שמועיאל מטטרין יהואל

פזק שקו צית בשכמלו

אבג יתץ קרע שטן נגד יכש בטר צתג חקב טנע יגל

כמיל לבד

שדי
מטטרון
יהואל

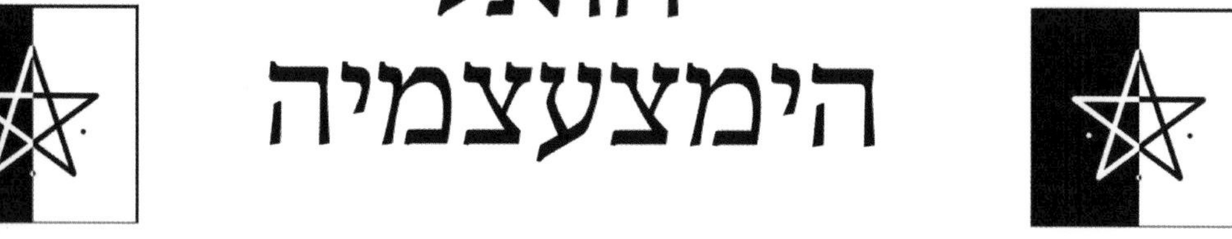

הימצעצמיה

א ט ד

ת ה ז

ד ה ד

תשגביבא טובאדא יה צורבא
תשגביבא טובאדא יה צורבא

ידהמובה

ד דודניאל
מ משפידאל
ב ביבאל

תשגביבא טובאדא יה צורבא
תשגביבא טובאדא יה צורבא

חיות אש ממללול

חיות אש ממללול חיות אש ממללול

כהת

אוריאל

בגיאן

הכת

חיות אש ממללול

חיות אש ממללול

רזיאל

Sisera

Labezerin

Eistibus

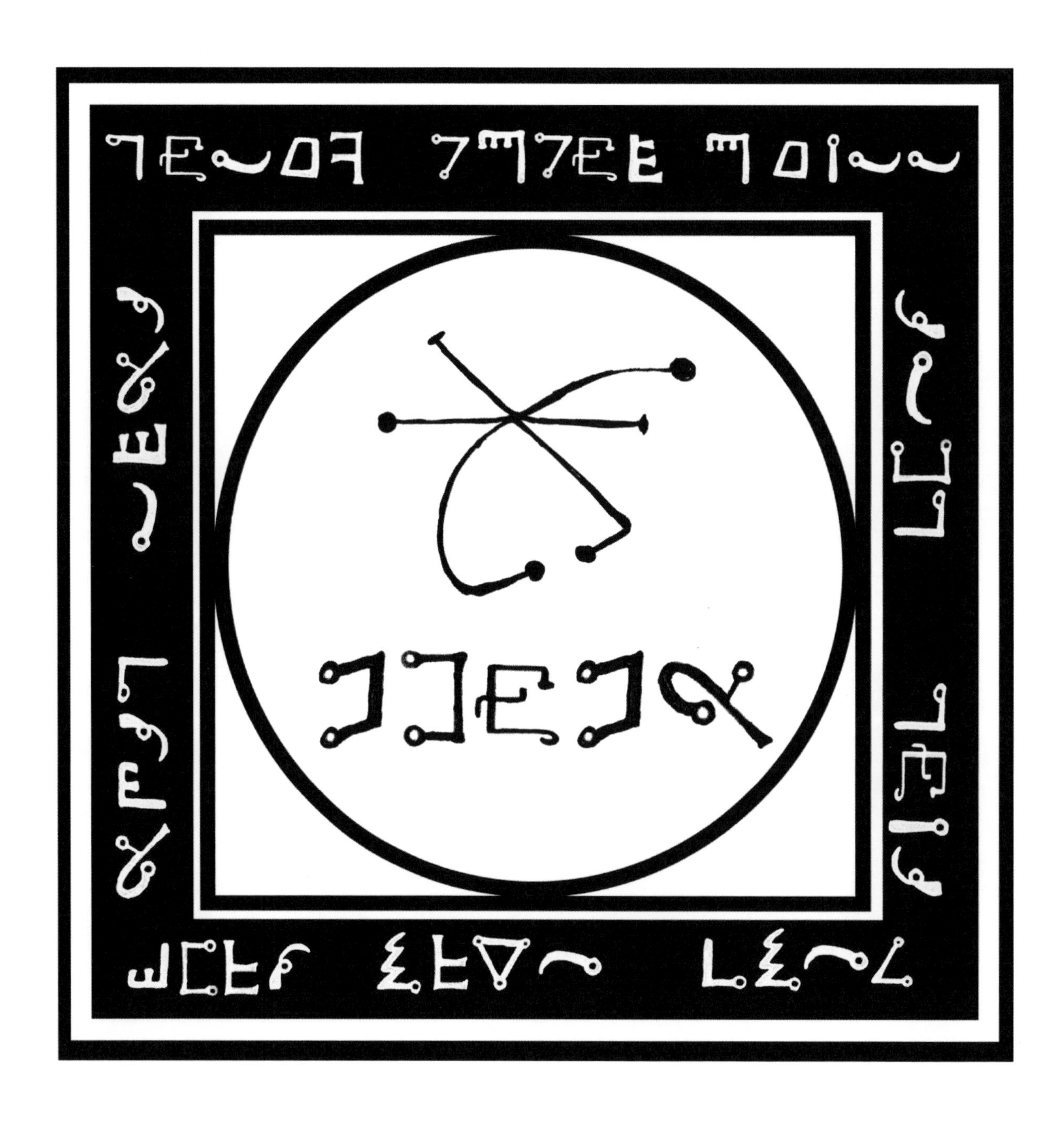

Nitika

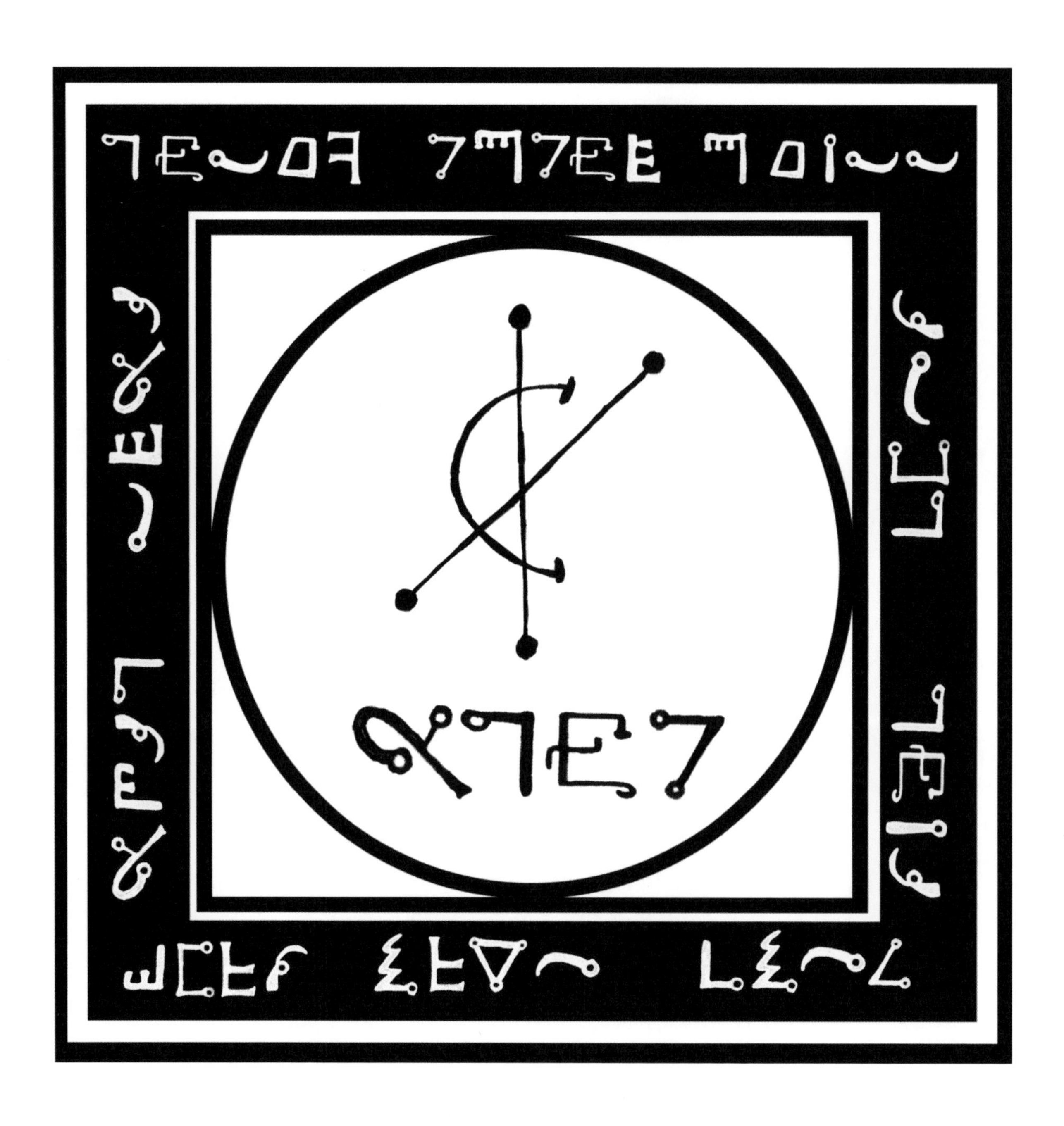

Haatan

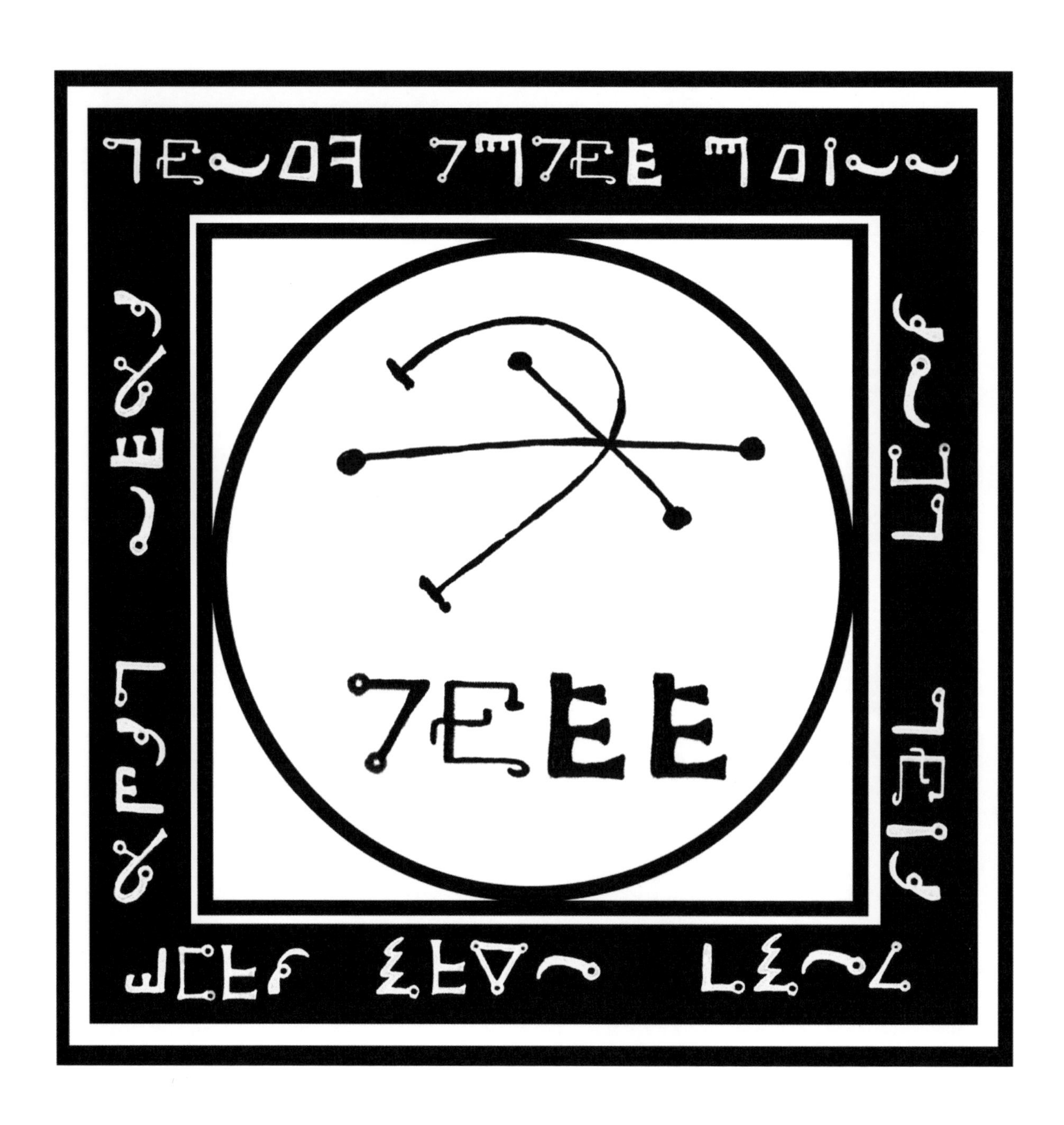

Sialul

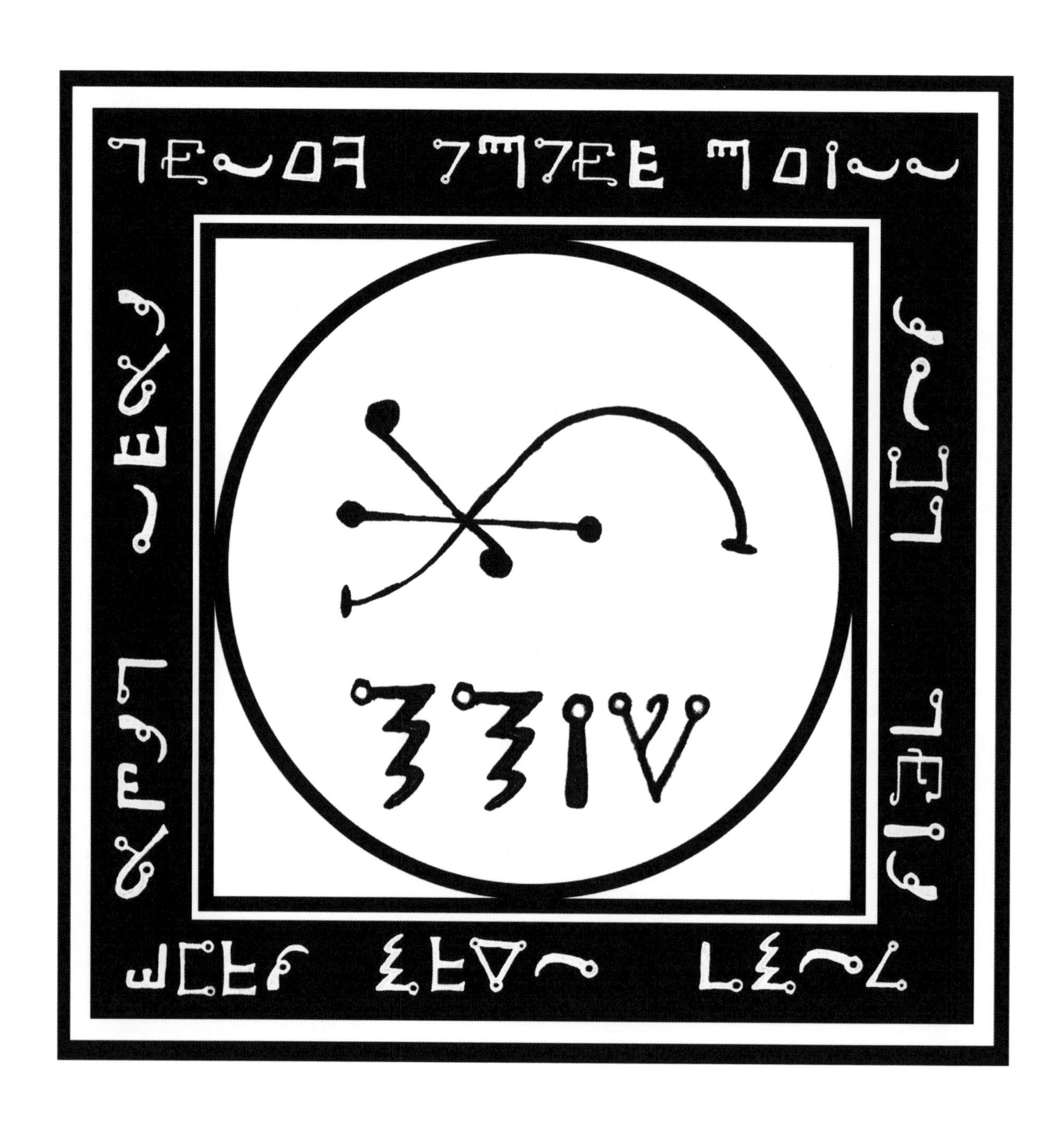

Librabis

Aeglun

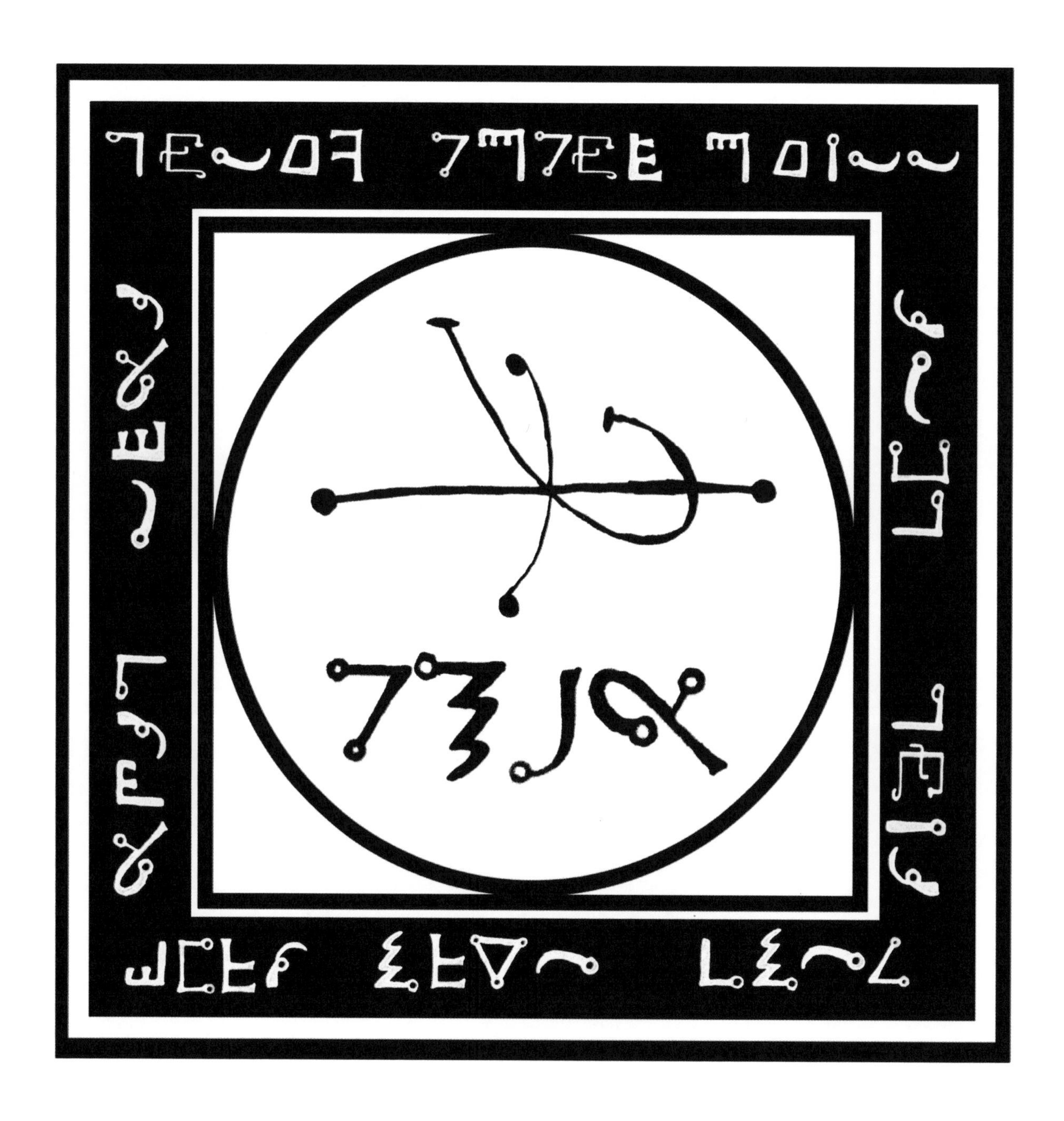

Butatar

Aclahayr

Toglas

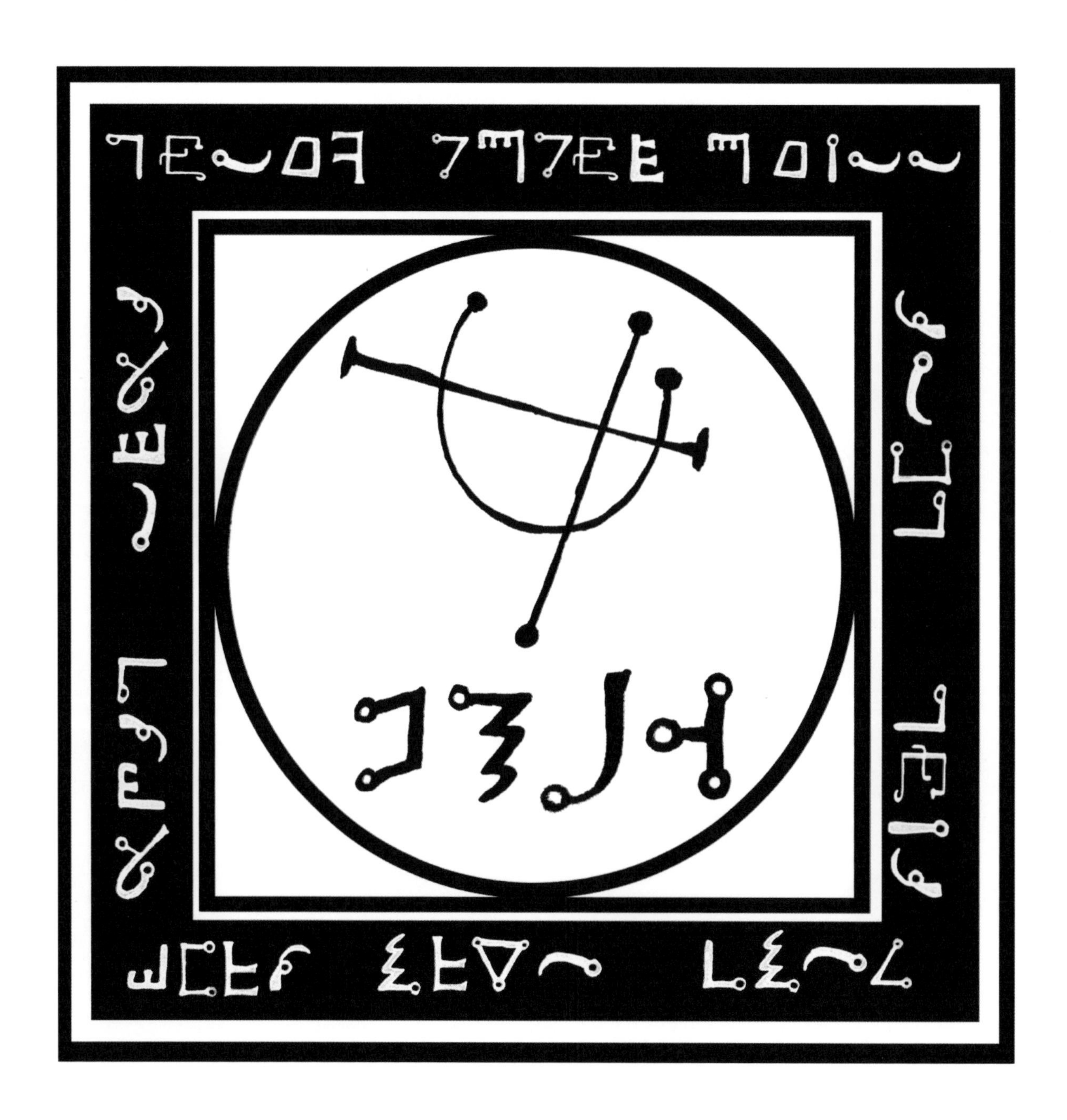

Images from Magickal Protection

The images can and should be used exactly as described in *Magickal Protection*, but I also know that some people like to keep physical copies near them. After you use the ritual to Cleanse Any Space, for example, you may like to keep a copy of the sigil in the place that you have cleansed. After performing the ritual to Become Less Conspicuous, you may want to carry that sigil on your person. Such additions to the magick are not required, but I know that some people like to use this approach, and these copies should make that easier.

The Sword Banishing Activation

יוהך
YOHACH

כלך
KALACH

אבגיתצ
AVGEETATZ

קרעשטנ
CARASSTAN

נגדיכש
NAGDEECHESH

בתרצתג
BATRATZTAG

חקבטנע
CHAKVETNAH

יגלפזק
YAGLEFZOK

שקוצית
SHAKUTZIT

נצריאל
NATZAREE-ELL

עוזיאל
OZEE-ELL

The Master Protection Ritual

Remove Parasitic Beings

Cleanse Any Space

Protect Your Job

Protect Your Business

Protect Against Accidents

Protection From Stalkers

Protection Against Unwanted Attention

Stop A Known Enemy

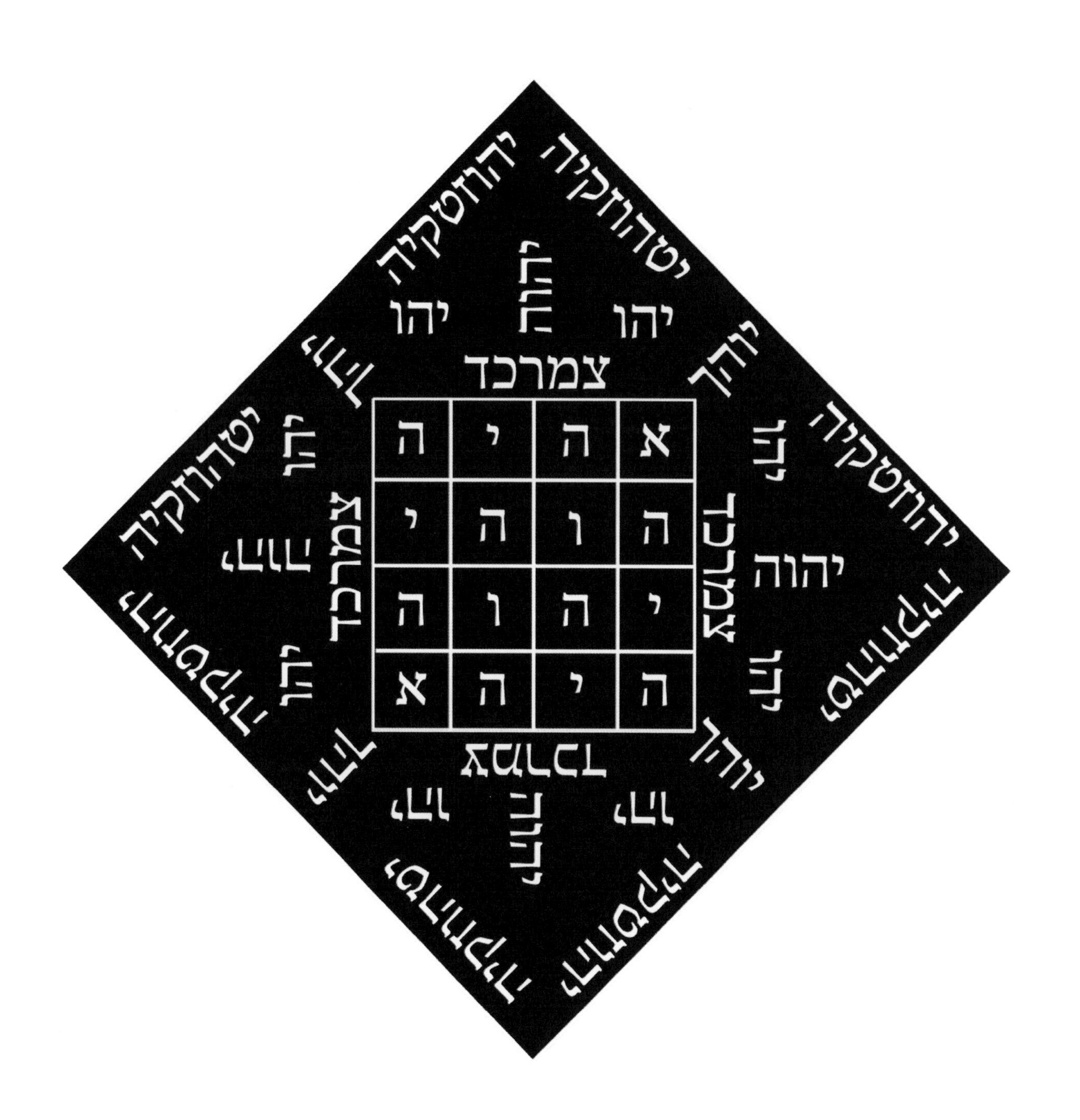

Stop a Known Enemy Part 2

Cancel a Curse or Supernatural Attack

Become Less Conspicuous

Protection Against Hacking and Identity Theft

Protection While Travelling

Protect Family and Loved Ones

Protection From Violence

Protection from Violence Part 2

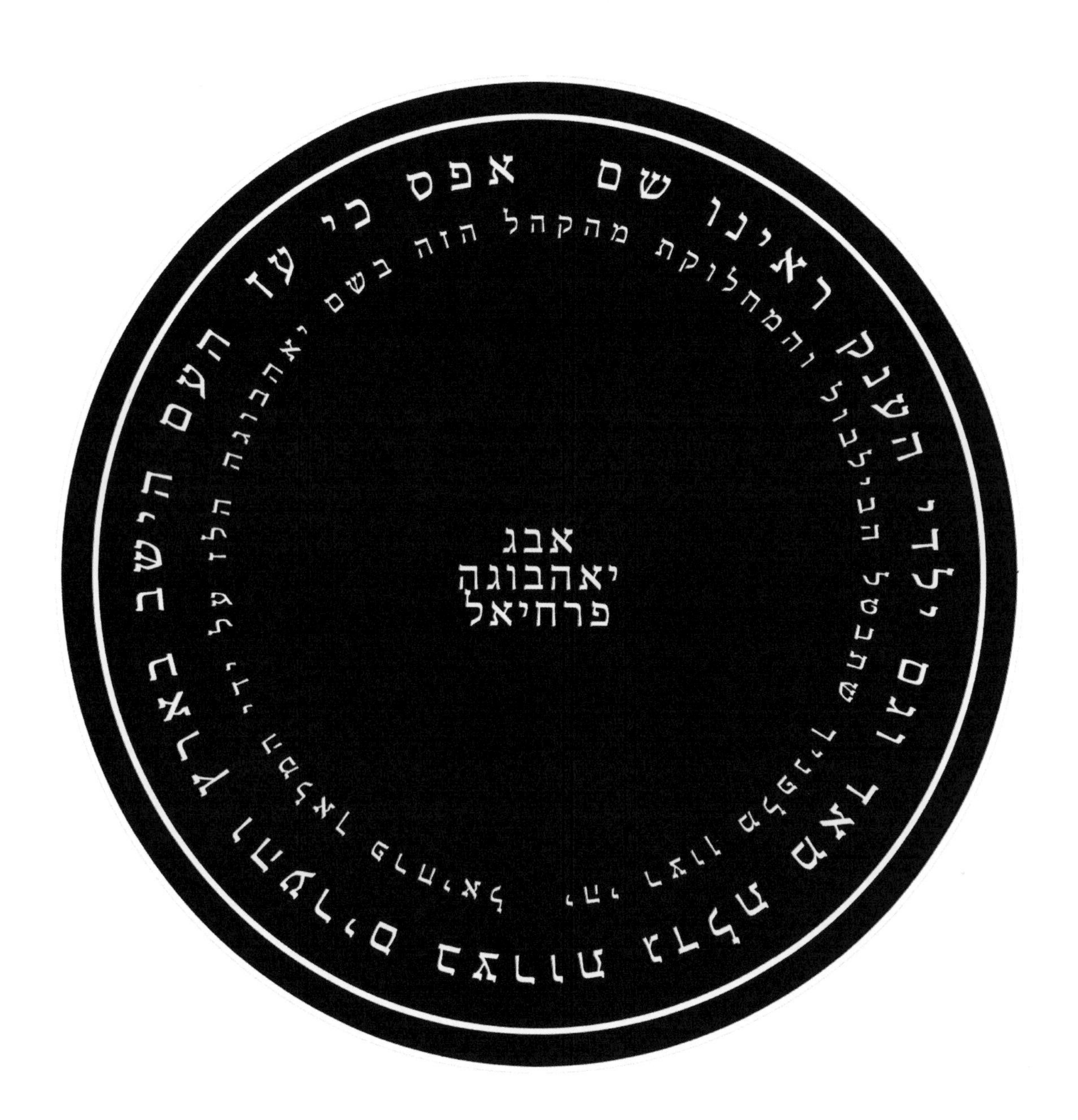

Stop Gossip and Rumours

Take Power From A Bully

Protect Your Home

Protect Your Possessions from Thieves

Protection Against Influence

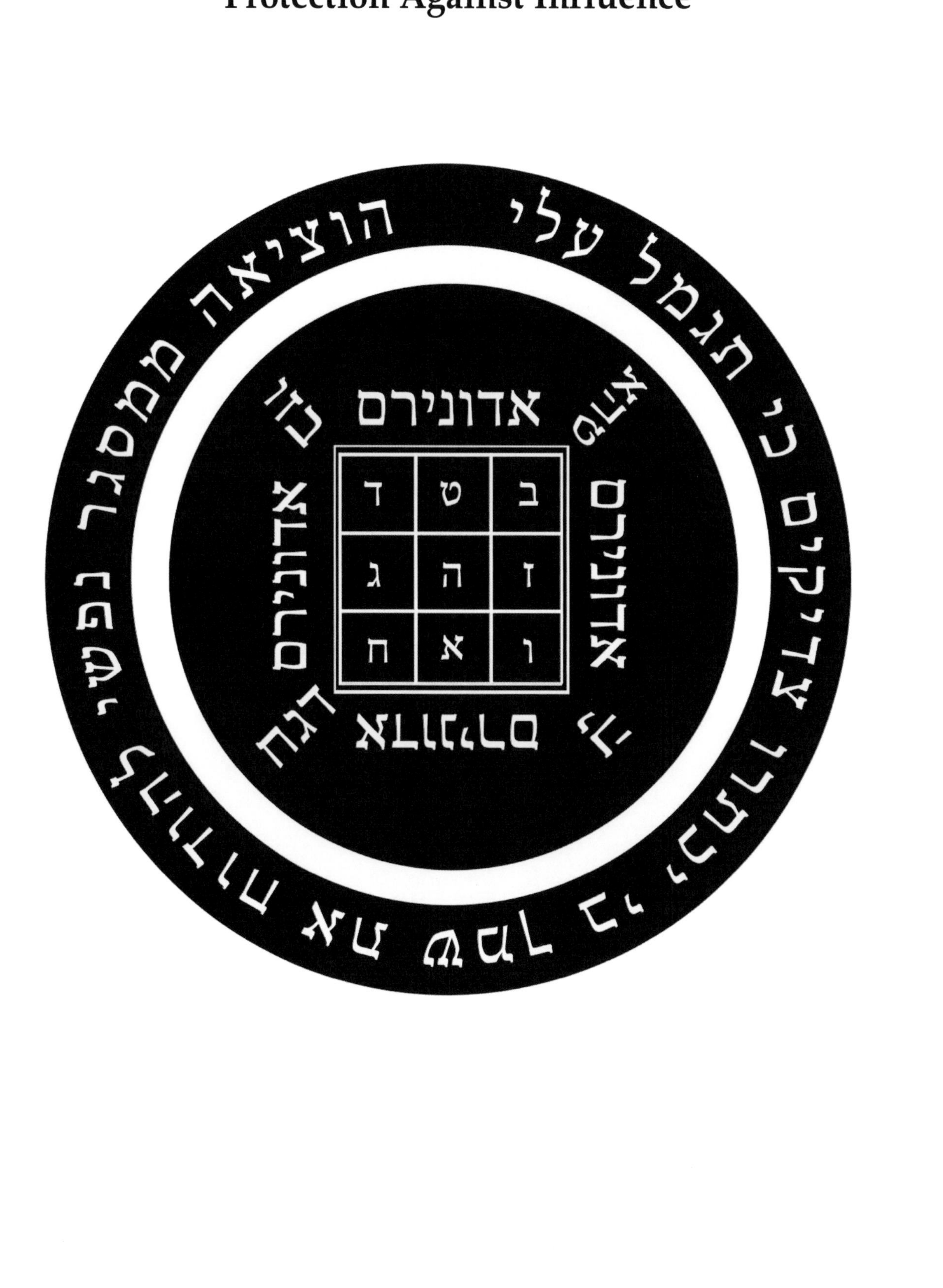

Images from Magickal Cashbook

The *Magickal Cashbook* requires that you place the Nitika sigil on the cover of your cashbook, with a second sigil on the back. They can be cut out and glued onto your book.

There are two additional versions here, which contain the correctly colored background, which can help the sigil blend in with your cashbook more effectively.

Nitika Sigil

Nitika Sigil Colored

Back Cover Sigil

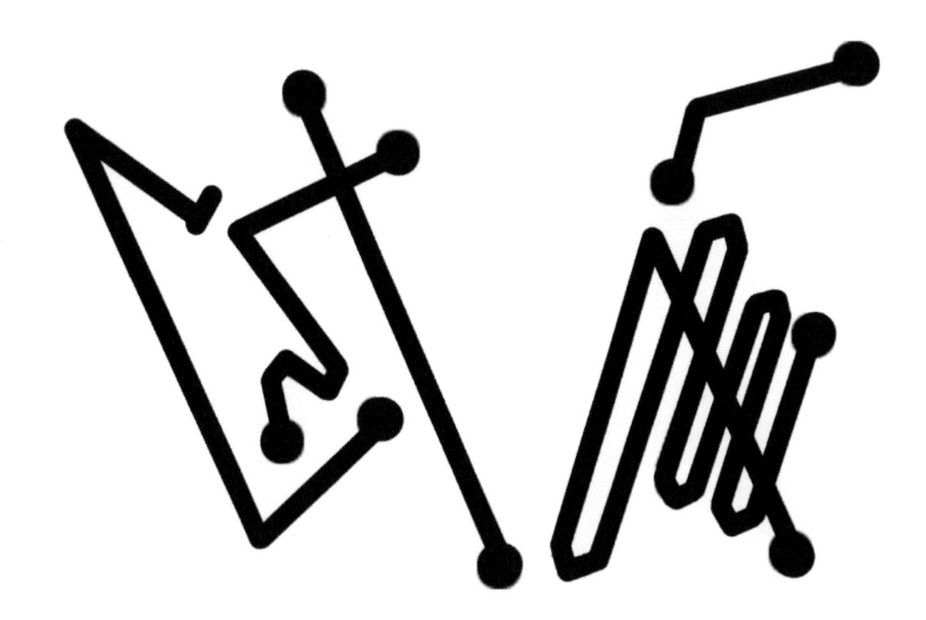

Back Cover Sigil Colored

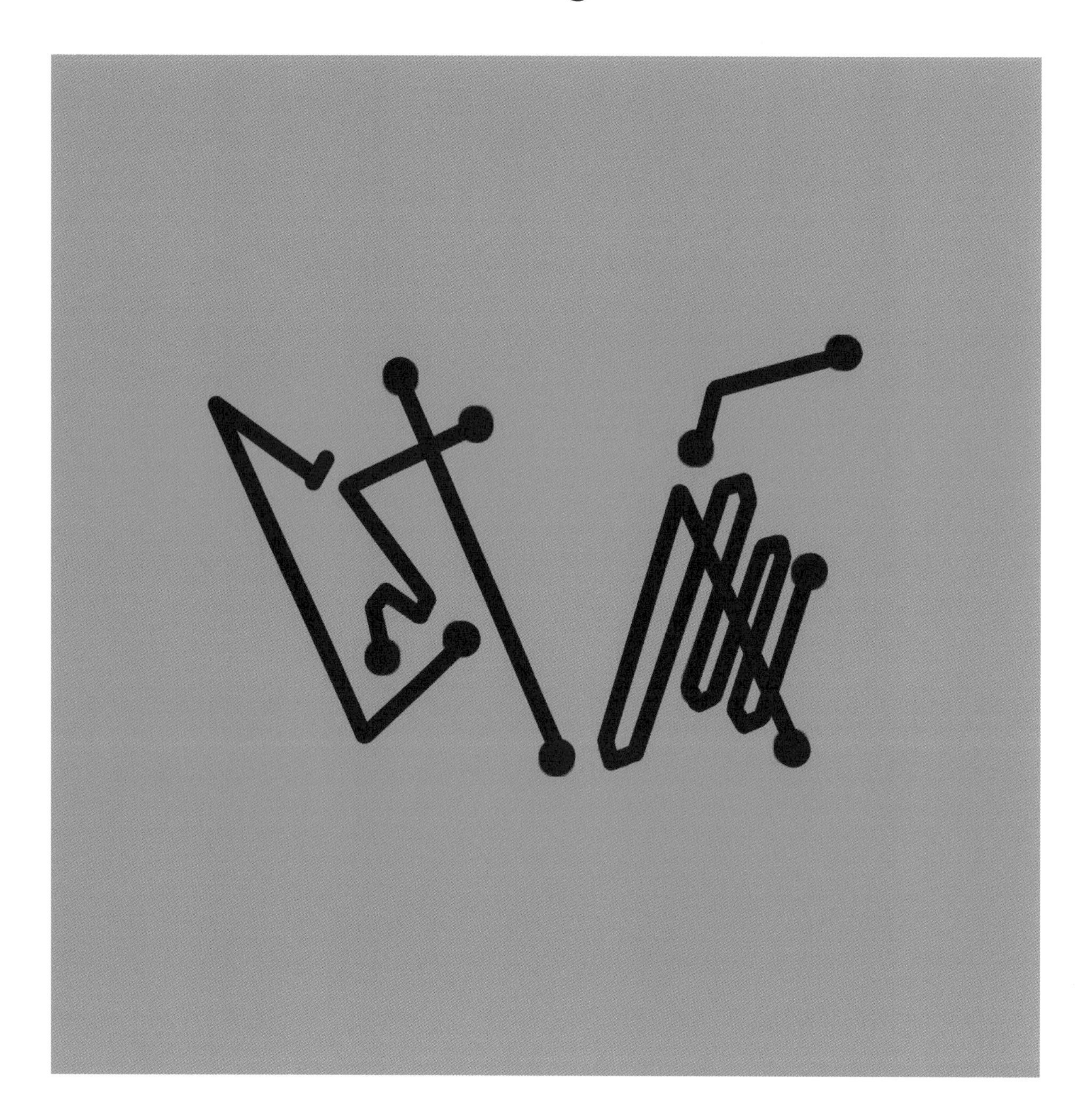

Printed in Poland
by Amazon Fulfillment
Poland Sp. z o.o., Wrocław